I0824563

A Sure Way

A Sure Way

Following Truth in a World on Fire

Edith Stein

Edited by Carolyn Beard
Introduction by Zena Hitz

Plough

Published by Plough Publishing House
Walden, New York
Robertsbridge, England
Elsmore, Australia
www.plough.com

Plough produces books, a quarterly magazine, and daily articles on Plough.com to encourage people and help them put their faith into action. We believe Jesus can transform the world and that his teachings and example apply to all aspects of life. At the same time, we seek common ground with all people regardless of their creed.

Plough is the publishing house of the Bruderhof, an international Christian community. The Bruderhof is a fellowship of families and singles practicing radical discipleship in the spirit of the first church in Jerusalem (Acts 2 and 4). Members devote their entire lives to serving God, one another, and their neighbors. They renounce private property and share everything. To learn more about the Bruderhof's faith, history, and daily life, see Bruderhof.com. (Views expressed by Plough authors are their own and do not necessarily reflect the position of the Bruderhof.)

Frontispiece photo courtesy of the Edith Stein Archive

ISBN 978-1-63608-176-2
29 28 27 26 1 2 3 4

A catalog record for this book is available from the British Library.

Library of Congress Cataloging-in-Publication Data

Names: Stein, Edith, Saint, 1891-1942 author | Beard, Carolyn editor
Title: A sure way : following truth in a world on fire / Edith Stein ; edited by Carolyn Beard.
Description: Walden, New York : Plough, [2026] | Includes bibliographical references. | Summary: "The Jewish philosopher who became a nun and died at Auschwitz guides the reader to the things that endure"-- Provided by publisher.
Identifiers: LCCN 2025035772 (print) | LCCN 2025035773 (ebook) | ISBN 9781636081762 trade paperback | ISBN 9781636081779 epub
Subjects: LCSH: Stein, Edith, Saint, 1891-1942 | Spiritual life--Catholic Apostolic Church
Classification: LCC BX4705.S814 A25 2026 (print) | LCC BX4705.S814 (ebook)
LC record available at https://lccn.loc.gov/2025035772
LC ebook record available at https://lccn.loc.gov/2025035773

Printed in the United States of America

Contents

Who Was Edith Stein? *vii*
Carolyn Beard
Reading Edith Stein Today *xviii*
Zena Hitz

Part I: Ways to Know God

1. Approaching God 3
2. Standing Before God 9
3. The Soul's Way to God 16
4. Hidden in God 19
5. On Christian Philosophy 22

Part II: At the Foot of the Cross

6. Juxta Crucem Tecum Stare 31
7. The Meaning of the Cross 33
8. Signum Crucis 41
9. The Dark Night of the Soul 44
10. The Night of Faith 51

Part III: Light Breaks In

11. Easter Morning 59

12. The Mystery of Sacrifice 61

13. The Holy Face 69

14. The Hidden Life and Epiphany 72

15. Holy Night 79

16. The Summons of Christmas 82

Part IV: Women's Spirituality

17. The Soul of Woman 95

18. Male and Female in the Image of God 100

19. Women's Destiny 103

Part V: A World in Flames

20. Holy Resistance 113

21. The Way of the Cross 116

22. The World Is in Flames 120

23. I Will Remain with You 125

Sources 130

Notes 131

Who Was Edith Stein?

Carolyn Beard

> "The world is in flames. The conflagration can also reach our house. But high above all flames towers the cross. The flames cannot consume the cross.
>
> "The world is in flames. Are you impelled to put them out?
>
> "The eyes of the Crucified look down on you – asking, probing. What will you answer him?"

EDITH STEIN SAW the world in flames. A German-Jewish philosopher turned Catholic monastic, she witnessed the rise of the Nazi regime and experienced the oppression of Jews and other minorities under the totalitarian state. In April 1933, the same month that a Nazi decree forced her out of her teaching post, Stein wrote to Pope Pius XI, urging him to protest Nazi violence against Jews. Throughout the mid to late 1930s, cloistered in a Carmelite monastery in Cologne,

Germany, Stein wrote spiritual missives on finding light in dark times. And in April 1941, having been smuggled into the Netherlands and hiding behind cloister walls, Stein reflected on the meaning of the cross: "The world is in flames. Are you impelled to put them out?"

Because of her Jewish heritage, Edith Stein was ultimately arrested and deported. She was killed at Auschwitz on August 9, 1942. Following her death at the Nazi extermination camp and her subsequent beatification and canonization in the Roman Catholic Church, Stein is remembered as a "Holocaust martyr" and saint. Stein's wartime writings, some of which are included in this book, are a compelling testament to what it means to live a life of faith in dark times. Written from Stein's unique vantage as a Jewish-Christian monastic, these writings are also cutting reprimands of Christians who failed to advocate for or protect their Jewish brothers and sisters in their time of need.

Yet Edith Stein's life and legacy contain so much more than her victimhood or the circumstances of her death. During her lifetime, Stein witnessed multiple turning points in twentieth-century Europe: she saw the golden age of the Prussian monarchy, the battlefield tragedies of World War I, the hope and rapid decline of the interwar period, the terror of the Nazi regime, and the horror of the Holocaust. She wore many different hats during her life: she was Jewish and Catholic, philosopher and mystic, daughter and sister, student and colleague, teacher and translator, poet and public speaker, nurse and suffragette. Stein's many identities point to the complexity of a life spent in pursuit of truth.

EDITH STEIN WAS BORN on October 12, 1891, in Breslau, Germany, now Wrocław, Poland. She was raised in an observant but assimilated upper-middle-class Jewish family. The youngest of eleven children, seven of whom survived to adulthood, Stein had an auspicious birthday – she was born on Yom Kippur, the holiest day in the Jewish year. Stein experienced loss from an early age: when she was eighteen months old, her father died of a heat stroke while on a business trip, leaving his wife, Auguste, in charge of the household and family business. In the summers, the Stein family would vacation in their ancestral hometown in Upper Silesia and visit the Jewish cemetery where Stein's ancestors and four of her siblings who had died in infancy were interred.

As a child, Stein was small and pale with a lively and mercurial temperament, known for being obstinate, impertinent, and precocious. But even from a young age, she felt the depth of her inner life, what she called her "hidden world." She was acutely sensitive to the suffering of others. "I would lie awake for hours at night, and, in the dark, horror would press in upon me from every corner." What for her was a deep, formative experience of "hidden suffering," her relatives wrote off as "nerves." While Stein's inner world was brightened by entering school, she continued to develop a deep sense of her own interiority as she grew up.

As the family matriarch and breadwinner, Auguste Stein insisted that her daughters receive a rigorous education, wanting to provide them with opportunities she had been denied. When Edith's sister Rose, just a year and a half her senior, began school, Edith insisted on joining her. After an older sister advocated her case to school administrators, Edith was permitted to enroll in school a year early. Catching up to her classmates, Stein demonstrated an early aptitude for learning, with particular interests in history and German. She regularly placed at the top of her class, and she felt most "at home" when she was at school.

Throughout her school days, by all accounts, Stein retained her lively spirit and vivid imagination, and during this time, she developed a proclivity for daydreaming. Already as a child, she felt a longing for something greater. "I always foresaw a brilliant future for myself. I dreamed about happiness and fame, for I was convinced that I was destined for something great and that I did not belong at all in the narrow, bourgeois circumstances to which I had been born."

Already as a child, Stein became "fed up" with school. When one of her older sisters in Hamburg had a baby, Stein took the opportunity to assist the new mother as an opening to take a break from school. What was supposed to be a six-week visit turned into a ten-month stay. It was during this period, exposed to a new world and literature "not fit" for a young girl, that Stein lost her childhood faith. At the age of fourteen, she stopped praying and became an atheist.

Almost a year later, when Stein returned to Breslau, she knew that she wanted to continue her studies. Because of her time away, she was behind and had to engage in months of rigorous work to qualify for secondary school. After earning her spot, she performed well academically and was well regarded by her classmates. For Stein's graduation, her classmates wrote a poem in honor of the budding suffragette:

> Let woman equal be with man,
> So loud this suffragette avers,
> In days to come we surely can
> See that a cabinet post is hers.

At a time when women were rarely allowed to pursue higher education, Stein passed her matriculation exam in March 1911 and enrolled at the University of Breslau, becoming one of only a few female students in the philosophy department. Though originally planning to pursue a degree in psychology, she developed a deep interest in philosophy when she read Edmund Husserl's *Logical Investigations*. In 1913, she transferred to the University of Göttingen to study under Husserl, the father of modern phenomenology. As a member of the Göttingen circle, a network of students and scholars studying Husserlian phenomenology, Stein found a community of scholars and colleagues who would become her lifelong friends and collaborators.

Stein's studies were cut short with the start of World War I. Hoping to contribute to the war effort and longing to be a part of something greater than herself, she returned to Breslau and volunteered with the Red Cross. For six months, she provided palliative care to soldiers while serving as a nurse in a field hospital, offering support to the wounded from all sides of the conflict. Through this work, Stein witnessed the horrific consequences of modern warfare. After her service, she returned to study under Husserl, now at the University of Freiburg. In 1916, she earned her doctorate in philosophy with a dissertation on empathy, and went on to serve as Husserl's research assistant, compiling and expanding his chaotic notes. Though Stein wanted to build a career as an academic, her gender barred her from access, since she was unable to find a faculty willing to accept her for the next stage of her education. After she petitioned her cause, Prussian authorities formally banned gender discrimination in the academic advancement process.

It was in this season of significant social and personal change that Stein had a conversion experience. Though raised in an observant Jewish family, she had renounced her childhood faith as a teenager. While a young adult away at university, Stein occasionally observed Jewish holidays with the gift packages her mother mailed from home. Even after her conversion to Christianity, she maintained a positive relationship with Judaism as her heritage and cultural inheritance, particularly expressing deep compassion for and solidarity with Jewish communities.

Stein does not offer a single, cohesive narrative of her conversion to Christianity. Instead, across her personal writings, she leaves a collection of short, illustrative impressions that reflect her gradual movement toward faith. She recalls a moment in 1911 when, while attending the University of Breslau, she and a friend visited one of Breslau's historic churches adjoining the university during a free period. When she moved to the University of Göttingen, Stein became colleagues and friends with a wide circle of Protestant and Catholic philosophers.

In July 1916, Stein took a trip to visit a fellow philosopher in Frankfurt am Main. She was deeply moved by the Christian funereal iconography she saw at a museum. And when she visited the city's cathedral, she witnessed a woman set down her market basket to kneel and pray. Reflecting on the impact this moment had on her faith journey more than a decade later, Stein wrote that it was as if the woman was engaged in an "intimate conversation" with God. Stein's autobiography makes clear what a deep impression this chance encounter left on her.

In 1921, when visiting friends and fellow philosophers Theodor and Hedwig Conrad Martius, Stein read the biography of mystic Saint Teresa of Ávila and felt that she had finally encountered the truth. On January 1, 1922, Stein was baptized into the Catholic Church. Though she initially wanted to enter monastic life, spiritual advisors encouraged her to serve God and the church in an academic career. She spent the following decade working as a teacher, writer, and lecturer, training educators, writing essays, and delivering lectures on Catholic and women's education. In reflections after her death, Stein's former students recalled her as an exacting but generous instructor who helped them develop a lifelong love for learning.

With the Nazis' rise to power in 1933 and the prohibition against the employment of Jews in civil service that April, Stein lost her teaching position at a public university. She wrote a letter to Pope Pius XI, appealing to their shared Christian values and calling on Rome to protest the mounting violence against Jews. Stein's letter was received by the Vatican but was not answered. The letter attests to her complicated Jewish-Christian identity and passionate empathy for the suffering of others; it is also part of a larger body of evidence that points to the failure of Christian institutions to protect Jewish people during the Nazi period.

Having been removed from her professional employment, Stein's path was cleared to enter monastic life. For the last decade of her life, she lived behind cloister walls. In 1935, Stein professed her monastic vows at the Carmelite monastery in Cologne, where she took on the name Teresa Benedicta of the Cross, a name that points to her intellectual and spiritual relationships with Teresa of Ávila and John of the Cross. Because of the economic crisis in Germany, when Stein took her final vows, she wore a wedding dress borrowed from her university friend and fellow philosopher Hedwig Conrad Martius. Though not employed as an academic, Stein continued to be an incredibly prolific writer in the monastery, penning essays, translations, liturgical texts, and poetry.

As conditions for Jews in Germany worsened, Stein's safety in Cologne became precarious. Following the widespread violence against Jews across Germany the night of November 9, 1938, a pogrom that came to be known as Kristallnacht, Stein feared that her presence would jeopardize the safety of the monastery and her religious sisters. On New Year's Eve 1938, she was smuggled over the German border and taken into hiding in a Carmelite monastery in the Netherlands. Ultimately, Edith Stein was arrested in the Netherlands on August 2, 1942. She was moved between Nazi transit camps and finally transported to Auschwitz, where she died in the gas chamber on August 9.

Because of her murder in the Holocaust, Edith Stein is remembered as one among the millions of victims of the Nazi regime. But her life and writings attest to much more: her pursuit of truth, her journey to faith, and her resistance to a totalitarian regime. The following pages contain a sampling of Stein's most intimate writings.

While these texts range from the philosophical to the poetic, they each invite us to walk in faith with her: to seek the truth, to deepen our inner lives, and to draw closer to God.

Carolyn Beard is a minister and PhD candidate in religion at the University of Toronto. A graduate of Princeton University and Harvard Divinity School, she has had her research on Edith Stein's political resistance published in Sojourners, The German Diplomat, *and* Edith Stein Jahrbuch.

Reading Edith Stein Today

Zena Hitz

WHY READ EDITH STEIN TODAY? She herself tells us why, in the following pages:

> What is, then, the great sickness of our time and people? There is an inner disunion, a complete deficiency of set convictions and strong principles, an aimless drifting. Therefore, the great mass of humanity seeks an anesthetic in ever new, ever more refined delights. Those who wish to maintain a sober level of life, in order to protect themselves from contemporary turmoil, frequently annihilate this level by one-sided professional work; but even they cannot do anything to escape the turmoil.

We members of "the great mass of humanity" – or at least a narrower group, the global middle class and those who aspire to it – find ourselves caught between addiction to pleasure and addiction to work. What clear goal organizes our lives? We live by media-driven trends and technological fads. We drift in the consumer markets. We are borne along on streams of public opinion whose basis in reality is questionable. Our attention is bought and sold by large companies unconcerned about our well-being or our contact with truth.

Why is the drifting painful? In part, because our own happiness depends on deep truths; unless those truths find us and we them, neither "refined delights" nor work can console us. Our desire for goodness and for real community is muffled and suppressed. Our modern media display in detail war, famine, and large-scale displacement. Yet our love and pity meet the obstacle of our own powerlessness. Our hearts long for a way of life that is steadfast and strong as well as ingenious and effective in the face of suffering.

Our governments are meant to effect the work of repair, but instead of a humane order we find a struggle between raw loci of power, none of which has any right to prevail over another. At one time, an appeal to ethical principles might have been offered as a fig leaf over naked self-interest. Now the mask has fallen away. The turmoil of these struggles for power is not an abstraction but bears real suffering in its wake: the suffering of those whose paths to a decent life have been erased, the suffering of the prisoner, the suffering of the migrant. Without strong common principles to cling to, we hide from the pain by pursuing the "refined delights" of artisanal cocktails or fine dining, mountain climbing or elaborately designed games.

Alternately – and here Stein has cut straight to my own heart – we bury ourselves in work, hoping there to find the seriousness that has been set adrift by the chaos of social life. Yet work does not give us strength nor saving grace. Our strength can come only from God. Stein continues:

> Only whole human beings . . . are immune to the contemporary sickness: such beings are steadfast on eternal first principles, unperturbed in their views and in their actions by the changing modes of thoughts, follies, and depravities surrounding them. Every such individual is like a pillar to which many can fasten themselves, thereby attaining a firm footing.

Those anchored in Jesus Christ can provide a hitching post for others. Eternal first principles, as Stein puts it, are our only hope.

Reading Edith Stein Today

I FIRST ENCOUNTERED Edith Stein, or Saint Teresa Benedicta of the Cross, while preparing for baptism – along with the rites of confirmation and first communion – in the Roman Catholic Church. I was thirty-two. It is traditional to receive one's confirmation with an appeal to a patron saint. I struggled to choose one. My godmother, a math professor, found Saint Teresa Benedicta and passed on some of her writings. My godmother's thinking was obvious: I, like Stein, was a philosophy professor with a Jewish background.

I found Stein's writing formidable and difficult to like. Much of it bears the stamp of the German academic world that educated her. The voice is passive, the language abstract, the aim scientific. Even her spiritual writing, while profound, is sometimes austere and impersonal. She keeps her own heart hidden. But stay with her long enough, and you will be rewarded.

By the obstacles she presents to her readers, Stein resembles the great Carmelite sister Thérèse of Lisieux, who was canonized during Stein's lifetime. Thérèse's writing bears the stamp of a French bourgeoisie soaked in sentimentality. Its profound truths lie behind a veil of saccharine sweetness. Yet Thérèse is a fearsome saint; once her teaching is understood, it can inspire something like terror and awe at the holy strength and brilliance of this young woman. The theologian Hans Urs von Balthasar compares the fierceness of Thérèse to that of Saint Paul: two saints with whom a personal encounter might inspire holy dread.

Stein, too, is a saint who can inspire such holy dread. Her natural strength and accomplishments contribute to the effect. Stein's mother was a powerful business owner; Stein herself was a suffragette and a successful academic at a time when women were generally excluded from those halls. Her embrace of humility, first as a Catholic, and then as a nun, must have been hard won. Her divine strength, given by grace, hides behind her formidable natural character. Once glimpsed, however, the strength of the nun and martyr dwarfs the merely human strength on which she relied in her early life, and whose vestige remains on her writing. The philosophy student who could not find employment because of her gender needed fierce human strength; the woman who chose to enter the Carmelites and later faced the death camps could only have done so by divine grace.

As I have spent more time with Stein's writing, I have found that what appears cold and impersonal at first turns out to be passionately universal. Under the veil of academic and monastic austerity is a heart burning with love and tenderness. Stein's philosophical bent gives her spiritual writing a powerful objectivity and breadth of scope that a personal memoir might miss.

Stein's last work, *The Science of the Cross*, excerpted here, was left open on her desk when she was arrested and taken to Auschwitz. Its writing is contemporary with the memoir of Etty Hillesum, a young Dutch Jewish woman who met the same fate. From Hillesum we can learn what it might feel like, from one day to the next, to face such a death and choose to offer it to God. By a strange coincidence, Hillesum was a volunteer at the transit camp of Westerbork when the transport carrying Stein passed through. As far as we know the two never met. Hillesum's letters describe the effect the transport of Catholic priests and religious had on those in the camp. Another witness reported seeing Stein at the camp, consoling parents and helping to look after their small children.

By contrast to Hillesum, we learn little of Stein's experiences from her writing. In her last writings, she reaches into the teachings of the great Carmelite reformer Saint John of the Cross. The "science of the cross" – a deceptively academic-sounding phrase – turns out to be a living seed, not a "science" or a body of true statements in the least. The cross is not a mere image or historical event. It is alive, growing and working through the hearts of the faithful:

> [The cross is] a living, real, and effective truth. It is buried in the soul like a seed that takes root there, making a distinct impression on the soul, determining what it does and omits, and by shining outwardly is recognized in this very doing and omitting.

Here again, the philosophical language veils a concrete reality. Christians walk in the shadow of the cross; Christian saints display this cross in their lives. Consider Stein's own "doing and omitting." When fired from her post in 1933 for her Jewish background, she did not emigrate to a lucrative teaching career in the United States. Instead, she became a Carmelite nun in the country that was seeking to bind and corner her. She was not reckless; when her community and her life were threatened, she emigrated to a convent in the Netherlands. When the Gestapo pursued her even there, she chose to suffer and die along with many thousands of others.

The shape of Stein's life is cruciform, and she tells us why: the seed of grace planted in her heart grew and gave her the capacity to sacrifice as Christ did.

AS THE WORLD AROUND HER turned from brutality and repression into the flames of war, Stein posed a question to her Carmelite sisters – and perhaps to her own suffragette heart that sought strength in action: "The world is in flames. Are you impelled to put them out?"

Our own age is an age of problem-solving. We seek data-driven solutions to famine, war, illness, and corruption. As I write, these solutions are being unveiled as spectacular failures. War has spread rather than contracted. Famine and disease are on the upswing. Governments abandon the semblance of principle and do as they please against whatever enemies they choose to pursue.

Addressing her sisters in the convent days after the German and Soviet invasions of Poland, Stein appeals to the natural desire to aid the wounded and console the dying. Yet, Stein says, the faithful observance of their vows, the humble life of prayer and service in community, is more than sufficient. By union with Christ, "you are omnipresent as he is. . . . You can be at all fronts, wherever there is grief, in the power of the cross."

Writing of the value of a woman in ordinary life, she points out that "everywhere she meets with a human being, she will find opportunity to sustain, to counsel, to help." She sees in the most ordinary circumstances of life a canvas on which the cross of Christ can bring salvation. Our role is not dramatic on its face. The drama is the divine action. We need only to pray, serve, and suffer with fidelity.

We can read Stein's words and imagine what she does not describe for us: the crucifixion of her own ambition. But her advice is also perceptive and prudent. Our role is not to govern the world, but to love one another. Such love is humble, small, and often invisible, and yet the health of the world hinges on it.

EDITH STEIN BEGAN her adulthood as a philosopher, a seeker of wisdom and understanding. Edmund Husserl, her teacher, sought to steer philosophy back to the encounter with truth that modern scientific thought had obscured. Such intellectual work must seem a long way from God, and certainly the furthest thing from the humble acts of service Stein was seen doing up until her last moments.

Stein the philosopher saw the simple Christian argument as if it were addressed to her personally: philosophy strives for wisdom, but we cannot achieve wisdom by our own powers. Christ is wisdom, as Paul preaches in the First Letter to the Corinthians. Faith in

Christ is offered to everyone, and in fact seems to come more readily to the humble than to philosophy professors. The perfect fulfillment of the search for wisdom is the sight of God in the afterlife.

Stein leaves it to us to draw out the scandal presented by her own life. She began her pursuit of wisdom as a favored student of Edmund Husserl, arguably the greatest philosopher of his time. She concluded it after spending some years behind the walls of a convent, following a simple rule of work and prayer, and then submitting to the grotesque humiliation of industrial-scale murder.

Wisdom is not to be found in the halls of power nor in the halls of scholarship. It is found, by the reception of grace, in the depths of the human heart. There, through the action of the living and almighty cross of Christ, we find the scope for action we have always longed for. We walk in the footsteps of an executed criminal. Through that execution, sufficient light and grace have been poured out to illuminate all the darkness of our world. Because Christ died for us, the care of a small child can be a wedge of grace sufficient to smash the structure of mass murder.

As the long Carmelite tradition famously teaches, the light of Christ sometimes comes to us in the form of thick darkness. God lovingly weans us from our dependence on dramatic displays of divine power and on palpable consolations. He leads us on to greater and greater leaps into the dark. Christ tells doubting Thomas that those who do not see yet still believe are more blessed. The invitation for the Christian is not to turn away from darkness but to face it, with courage and with a heart overflowing with love.

I grew up in the 1970s, when the memory of the Holocaust was still fresh. My grandmother fled Europe with her family in the 1930s. Her own grandmother was murdered in Poland with other members of our family. The death camps were, for my generation, the image of the pinnacle of human evil. The spirit under which we were taught about the camps and their ruling regime was one of humility: born in different circumstances, we might have been the perpetrators. I could never have imagined, in my pre-Christian life, that someone might have been capable of facing down the death camps. Who could look at them squarely and say to God, "Not my will, but thine be done"?

It is easy to see why I would have found this hard to imagine, as strength of this kind is not humanly given. It is, rather, the culmination of a life lived in open and willing dependence on grace. As we face the darkness of our own age, there is no more fitting companion than the philosophy-professor-turned-nun who looked the deepest evil in the eye and leaped, trusting all to the God who made the heavens and the earth.

Zena Hitz is a tutor at St. John's College, the founder of The Catherine Project, and the author of Lost in Thought: The Hidden Pleasures of an Intellectual Life *and* A Philosopher Looks at the Religious Life.

PART I

Ways to Know God

I

Approaching God

God often seems absent, but Edith Stein reminds us that God always desires to be in relationship with us. In her posthumously published 1941 essay "Ways to Know God," from which the following two readings are excerpted, Stein considers the different ways people approach God, whether through nature, scripture, faith, or a direct experience of God's presence.

GOD WISHES to let himself be found by those who seek him. Hence, he wishes first to be sought. . . . Faith is already a finding and corresponds to God letting himself be found, not only in the sense that through his word God says something about himself but that through his word he also lets himself be found.

Faith is a gift that must be accepted. In faith, divine and human freedom meet. But it is a gift that bids us ask for more. As dark and lacking the evidence of insight, faith awakens a yearning for unveiled clarity; as mediated encounter, it awakens a longing for an immediate encounter with God. Indeed, the very content of faith awakens desire by promising the beatific vision.

THE PERSON WHO already possesses an experiential knowledge of God will have the most proper understanding. . . . However, a certain understanding is also quite possible on the basis of faith and even of the natural knowledge of God. The person who knows and loves God from and in his living faith will be eager to come to know him from ever-changing perspectives and in new features, and again and again he will turn to the Holy Scriptures that make this possible. . . .

When a person lacking faith reads Holy Scripture – for example, for the purposes of philology or religious studies – he does not come to know God. He only learns how God is conceived in the Bible and by those who accept the Bible in faith, unless faith is awakened in him by what he reads, but in this case there is a transition from one outlook to another.

Even within faith there are various ways of understanding and coming to know. The person reading Holy Scripture with faith accepts whatever he reads "in faith," that is, as revealed truth. But this on no account means that he grasps everything in a *living way* that affects his *soul*. His reading may be largely an empty grasp of the meaning of the words, without any effect on his life experience. We feel the difference clearly when all of a sudden we see a passage we have often read "in a new light" – in a light that shows us something about God that was hidden from us before or . . . in our own soul. We can also be affected in a quite personal way by a divine demand that we did not realize before. Or a new relationship among truths of faith that until now were unconnected may strike us.

All this is possible "in the light of faith." Our knowledge of God is enriched by it, our relationship with God deepened and better ordered; yet with faith we still do not stand before God himself. But this, too, may happen: a word of Scripture may so touch me in my innermost being that in this word I feel God himself speaking to me and sense his presence. The book and the sacred writer, or the preacher that I was just hearing, have vanished – *God himself is speaking*, and he is speaking to *me*. At the time, the ground of faith is not exactly left behind, but for the moment I am raised above it to the experiential knowledge of God.

This is, at bottom, the goal of all theology: to clear the way to God himself. . . . Theology addresses a select group, and for its adherents – that is, for those who have already experienced a certain enlightenment and hence are striving for holiness – it would do more than instruct them in the content of faith. By unveiling a suprasensible world for them through its images, it would teach them to free themselves more and more from the world of the senses and, in the end, it will bring them to the point where they no longer need sensible images at all. It will "lead them by the hand" first from the sensible to the spiritual and suprasensible, and finally to the highest summit, to oneness with the One. This last stage, of course, lies not within the power of symbolic theology, but is God's affair; theology can but lead in the right direction.

Now, when we call experiential knowledge a "fulfillment" of faith, the term includes the notion that faith aims at the same thing that comes as given in experiential knowledge. This is a general feature of the relation of "intention" and "fulfillment." When I see something with my own eyes that I only heard about before – for example, a famous work of art or a beautiful city – the reality I now have before me already existed in my mental world. It had reached me in a certain way through what I was told or read, and I was already inwardly stirred by it.

And this is all the more true of faith. Holy Scripture counts as "God's Word" for us because therein he draws near to us, makes himself known to us, makes his demands upon us. Of course, the word is spoken "in his name" only so long as I take it purely on faith. God is not sensibly present, nor does he speak in his own person. And yet I do come into contact with him through this transmitted word, and by it I am inwardly moved. And this property of faith of going beyond itself – Saint Thomas calls faith "the beginning of eternal life in us" – is just what brings us to "know God again," to recognize him when he suddenly makes his presence felt or even when he shows himself visibly, and it is what enables us to understand, even without any experiential knowledge of our own, what others speak of from their experience of God.

What we have said here of faith may apply in a certain way to the natural knowledge of God. A person who has grown up without religious instruction but is sensitive to the traces of God in nature, in his own heart, and in human life may perceive his failings as "sins" and a loss he suffers as "God's punishment." He can appreciate it when God is said to flare up in anger and to be a consuming fire. However imperfect and vague his natural knowledge of God may be, however much it needs to be corrected and enriched, clarified and explained by faith, it already points to what will become reality in the experiential knowledge of God. Also, in the natural knowledge of God, a certain encounter with God takes place that enables him to "know him again, to recognize him," should God ever stand before him.

2

Standing Before God

As a mystic, Edith Stein is not satisfied to know about God or accept him in faith, but desires to experience his presence and, some day, to stand before him face to face.

WHAT MAKES THE PROPHET certain that he is standing before God? Seeing with the eyes or in the imagination does not necessarily have anything to do with this. When both are absent, there may still be an inner certainty that it is God who is speaking. This certainty can rest on the "feeling" that God is present; one feels touched in one's innermost being by him, by the One present. We call this the *experience* of God in the proper sense. It is the core of all mystical living experience: the person-to-person encounter with God. A sensible vision, like that of Isaiah, may accompany it as an extraordinary attendant phenomenon.

On the other hand, is a vision like this conceivable without a personal inner experience of God? It is not impossible that the prophet could see the Lord before him or hear his words without being inwardly touched by him in mystical fashion. This is obviously the case with the boy Samuel, who hears God calling him without realizing that it is God calling. Hence, he does not recognize God. In Isaiah's case, we might say that the miraculous character of his apparition and the accord between what he sees and hears and what he knows about God from faith could convince him, without being inwardly touched, that it is God himself.

Although we should not dismiss this interpretation as impossible, it does seem to be a somewhat artificial construction. When we read that young Samuel did not yet know the Lord, it seems to me to suggest that Eli did know him and that Samuel was going to meet him. After Samuel received the revelation, we get the definite impression that he does know the Lord now – not from deductions and rational considerations but from a personal encounter, by being seized in his innermost being, from an encounter that stirred the child to become a prophet. In such a genuine living experience of receiving a mission, inspiration, revelation, and the consciousness of both are combined with a true experience of God. Many intermediate stages are possible between this fullness and the other extreme of receiving a revelation without knowing or willing it.

To begin anew from below, a person may be inspired and know he is inspired without receiving a revelation. The sacred writer knows that he is moved by God's Spirit to say or write something; how he expresses it may also be inspired and experienced as such. But what he has to communicate is not revelation for him. It may be events that he knows from experience or moral truths that he intuits with his natural understanding. (The historical and wisdom books of the Bible must, in part, have arisen in this way.)

The reverse – revelation without inspiration – we should say is impossible. Wherever God unveils himself or a hidden truth, he does so through his Spirit; and whenever a human being is chosen to convey such a truth to others, he must be guided by the Spirit. Divine truth may enlighten him as a purely intellectual truth, without his hearing any words or seeing any objects. And the words in which he casts his message may be left up to him. Whenever he hears a revelation in words or is shown an image, all he may have to do is pass on the image or the words without understanding them himself. But the intellectual meaning can also be disclosed to him through inner enlightenment or words added to explain it.

THERE IS SOMETHING more than the natural knowledge of God in all these cases and something beyond faith as well, but there still may not always be a personal experiential knowledge of God. We should first question whether in all these cases we should speak of knowledge of God at all. We might say that any experience like this will always be taken as coming from God. When a divine truth appears cast in "supernatural light," I mean, clearly distinct from natural knowledge and breaking into its context, the light will be taken as "divine light."

When words are spoken or a figure is seen and the one speaking or appearing does not claim to be God himself but an angel or saint, he nonetheless comes as a messenger of God. The person receiving the revelation knows that he is undergoing divine action through the messenger – or through an "intellectual vision." (This applies to inspiration as well, as long as it is not of demonic origin.) Still, the affected person does not stand before the Lord; God remains the hidden God.

On the other hand, Isaiah looked upon God himself and heard his word, and if our reading of his account is correct, he became certain in his innermost being that

God himself was present. Only when this happens may we speak of a personal experiential knowledge of God.

We call this "feeling of God's presence" the core of all mystical experience. However, it is only the beginning of the mystical life of prayer, the lowest stage. There are various degrees and transitions between this feeling and the summit of "infused contemplation," the lasting union with God. Each higher stage represents a richer, deeper self-revelation and self-commitment of God to the soul, and for the soul it means an ever deeper and fuller penetration into God and acquaintance with him, which demands from the soul an ever more total surrender.

Unlike revelations in which God does not disclose himself but only unveils a single truth or a single event inaccessible to natural knowledge, personal experiential knowledge is marked by an immediacy, in the sense that what is present itself is said to be experienced immediately, not what is merely grasped through its effects or made present by messengers. But God is not "immediately intuited" in the same way as something falling under the senses or even as something the mind knows by insight.

We call the personal encounter with the Lord the "experience of God" in the most proper sense. However, the kinds of indirect knowledge we mentioned should also be counted as supernatural experience and thereby distinct from faith. All forms of supernatural experience – but especially personal acquaintance – relate to faith in the same way that, in the natural realm, our own experience relates to knowledge based only on what we are told: as the *fulfillment* of what we previously grasped only intellectually without our own perception.

Personal encounter as fulfillment also contrasts with indirect experiential knowledge in the sense that what is itself known as present gives fulfillment to what is only indirectly known or made present. Moreover, personal encounter accords no final fulfillment either, but merely points beyond itself to a truer fulfillment in higher mystical experience and eventually in the beatific vision. . . .

We should compare the transition from knowing God naturally to experiencing him supernaturally to meeting a human being personally whose existence we previously only sensed in certain effects or perhaps gathered from these effects. Faith can serve as a bridge for this transition. Now, if we think of a transition from natural knowledge of God to a supernatural experience of God that is not mediated by faith, as when grace is bestowed on someone who lacked faith, and if this experience is "accepted," then the several kinds of fulfillment are therein combined, and the whole event will be much more strongly marked by inner disruption and transformation.

All kinds of knowledge of God are interconnected by the intentions through which they point beyond themselves, and in the final analysis – as long as we remain in earthly knowledge – are oriented toward the experience of God. This does not mean that natural knowledge of God and faith must precede supernatural experience, nor that they have their objective warrant therein. It means, rather, that there lies in them, according to their own essence, an aiming at the experience of God, as well as the possibility of their being found again transformed in that new way of knowledge.

3

The Soul's Way to God

Jesus says the way that leads to life is narrow and few find it. Edith Stein might add that the way to morning is through the night. Stein wrote The Science of the Cross, *from which the following passages are taken, between 1939 and 1942, while hiding from the Nazis in the Netherlands. She takes up the symbolic language of the night and the cross to consider how humanity might draw nearer to God through difficult times.*

GOD HAS CREATED human souls for himself. He desires to unite them to himself and to give them the immeasurable fullness and incomprehensible bliss of his own divine life, already in this life. That is the goal to which he directs them and toward which they themselves should strive with all their might. But the way to it is narrow, steep, and difficult. Most people remain en route. A few manage to get beyond the first beginnings – a dwindling small number arrive at the goal. That is due to the dangers on the way – worldly dangers, the evil enemy, and one's own nature – but also due to ignorance and lack of qualified guidance. Souls do not understand what is happening within them, and seldom is someone to be found who could open their eyes to what is going on. . . . Impassable barriers confront them on the way they have been traveling. But the new path that opens up before them leads through impenetrable darkness. Who has the courage to venture on it?

THE SPIRITUAL PRACTICES that up to now have been a source of inner joy become a torment, intolerably dull and fruitless. But there is no tendency to occupy oneself with worldly things. The soul desires above all else to remain still, without bestirring itself, allowing all its faculties to rest. But this seems to them to be sloth and a waste of time. That is more or less the state of the soul when God wishes to lead it into the dark night. In usual Christian parlance, such a condition will be called "a cross."

THERE IS NO immediately perceptible similarity between the cross and suffering, but neither is there a purely arbitrarily established relationship of symbols. The cross has acquired its meaning through its history.

It is not merely a natural object but rather a tool crafted and used by human hands for a very specific purpose. As a tool, it has played an incomparably important role in history. Everyone who lives in a Christian cultural sphere knows something about this role. Therefore, the cross in its visible form leads immediately to the fullness of meaning which is entwined with it. It is thus a symbol, but one that has not artificially gained meaning; rather, it has genuinely earned it by reason of its effectiveness and its history. Its visible form indicates the meaning connected with it.

4

Hidden in God

For Edith Stein, God also works in our lives in moments of stillness. In a 1936 essay, "The Prayer of the Church," written from the Carmelite convent in Cologne, she points to the hidden, quiet moments of our lives.

THE WORK OF SALVATION takes place in obscurity and stillness. In the heart's quiet dialogue with God, the living building blocks out of which the kingdom of God grows are prepared, and the chosen instruments for the construction forged. The mystical stream that flows through all centuries is no spurious tributary that has strayed from the prayer life of the church – it is its deepest life. When this mystical stream breaks through traditional forms, it does so because the Spirit that blows where it will is living in it, this Spirit that has created all traditional forms and must ever create new ones. Without it, there would be no liturgy and no church. Was not the soul of the royal psalmist a harp whose strings resounded under the gentle breath of the Holy Spirit? From the overflowing heart of the Virgin Mary blessed by God streamed the exultant hymn of the "Magnificat." When the angel's mysterious word became visible reality, the prophetic "Benedictus" hymn unsealed the lips of the old priest Zechariah, who had been struck dumb. Whatever arose from Spirit-filled hearts found expression in words and melodies, and continues to be communicated from mouth to mouth. The "Divine Office" is to see that it continues to resound from generation to generation.

So the mystical stream forms the many-voiced, continually swelling hymn of praise to the triune God, the Creator, the Redeemer, and the Perfecter. Therefore, it is not a question of placing the inner prayer free of all traditional forms as "subjective" piety in contrast to the liturgy as the "objective" prayer of the church. All authentic prayer is prayer of the church. Through every sincere prayer something happens in the church, and it is the church itself that is praying therein, for it is the Holy Spirit living in the church that intercedes for every individual soul "with sighs too deep for words" (Rom. 8:26). This is exactly what "authentic" prayer is, for "no one can say 'Jesus is Lord' except by the Holy Spirit" (1 Cor. 12:3).

What could the prayer of the church be, if not great lovers giving themselves to God who is love!

The unbounded loving surrender to God and God's return gift, full and enduring union: this is the highest elevation of the heart attainable, the highest level of prayer. Souls who have attained it are truly the heart of the church, and in them lives Jesus' high priestly love. Hidden with Christ in God, they can do nothing but radiate to other hearts the divine love that fills them and so participate in the perfection of all into unity in God, which was and is Jesus' great desire.

5

On Christian Philosophy

Written in the mid-1930s, shortly after Edith Stein entered a Carmelite convent, Finite and Eternal Being, *which explores the boundaries of faith, theology, and philosophy, is widely considered her magnum opus. In it, Stein invites her readers to engage in rigorous reflection to grow in faith.*

FAITH AND THEOLOGY enlighten natural reason as to the true nature of the *first existent*,[1] whom it had previously reached by its own efforts, and they also throw light on the relationship that exists between all that which is and the first existent. Natural reason could never have gained this illumination unaided. Reason would turn into unreason if it would stubbornly content itself with what it is able to discover with its own light, barring everything that is made visible to it by a brighter and more sublime light. For it ought to be emphasized that what is communicated to us by revelation is not

1 Stein uses the term "first existent" to refer to God as the first cause or prime mover.

something simply unintelligible but rather something with an intelligible meaning – a meaning, to be sure, that cannot be comprehended and demonstrated in the way natural facts are understood and demonstrated. What is communicated to us by revelation cannot be comprehended at all (that is, it cannot be exhaustively described by means of concepts) because it is in itself immeasurable and inexhaustible and at any time reveals only so much of its mystery as it wants us to understand. In themselves, however, the contents of revealed truth are supremely intelligible, and they become intelligible for us in the measure in which we receive light and with it the medium of a new understanding of natural facts, of which we now learn for the first time that they are *only* natural. . . .

The contents of revelation do not comprise the infinite plenitude of divine truth. God reveals himself to the human mind in a measure and manner commensurate with his wisdom. His sovereign will may see fit to enlarge this measure and to reveal the divine mysteries in a way commensurate with the modes of human thinking: with discursive reasoning, conceptual knowledge, and critical judgment. Or he may raise human beings above their natural ways of thinking to a totally different level of knowledge, making them partakers of that divine vision that embraces everything with one single and simple glance.

The perfect fulfillment of everything at which philosophy – as a striving toward wisdom – aims is the divine wisdom itself, the simple *visio* with which God embraces himself and all his creation. The highest perfection to which a created spirit may attain – but, to be sure, not without divine aid – is the *beatific vision.* This is the divine gift of union with God by which the created spirit partakes of divine knowledge in sharing divine life. The *mystical vision* or mystical union represents the closest approximation to this highest goal that is attainable in this earthly life. A preliminary stage, however, for which this highest favor is not required, is a true and living *faith*. . . .

Several elements are implicit in the act of faith: By accepting the truths of faith on the authority of God, we hold them to be true and we thereby give credence to God (*credere Deo*). But we cannot give credence to God unless we believe in God (*credere Deum*), that is unless we believe that God *is* and that he is *God*: We use the name God to designate the supreme and absolutely truthful being.

To accept the truths of faith means thus to accept God, for God is the real object of faith, and to him all the truths of faith are related. But to accept God also means to turn to him in our faith or to believe in God as the end of our faith (*credere in Deum*), that is, to strive toward God. Faith is thus a taking hold of God. This kind of seizing, however, presupposes a being seized. In other words, we cannot believe without divine grace. And grace means participation in divine life. Once we open ourselves to grace and accept the gift of faith, we have "within us the beginning of eternal life."

We accept faith on the testimony of God himself and thereby gain a certain knowledge without, however, obtaining a thorough comprehension. In other words, we cannot accept the truths of faith as evident in themselves as we do in the case of the necessary truths of reason or of the data of sense perception; nor can we deduce them logically from certain self-evident truths. This is one reason why faith is called a "dark light." Moreover, faith as a *credere Deum* and a *credere in Deum* always aspires beyond all revealed truth, that is, beyond all truth that God has confined in concepts and judgments, in words and sentences, in order to make it commensurate with the human mode of cognition. Faith asks of God more than individually separated truths: it desires God himself, all of him, who is truth, and it seizes him in darkness and blindness ("although it is night").

This night denotes the profound darkness of faith as compared with the eternal light to which it aspires. Saint John of the Cross refers to this dual darkness of faith when he writes, "In the course of the progress of the understanding, faith becomes stronger, and thus this progress brings on increasing darkness, since faith is darkness for the human reason." But it is an advancing, nevertheless, a going beyond all conceptually intelligible particularized knowledge to the simple comprehension of the one truth. Faith, therefore, is closer to divine wisdom than any philosophical or even theological knowledge or science. But because it is difficult to go forward in the dark, every ray of light that pierces our night gives us a glimpse of the future brightness and is therefore an invaluable aid in keeping us from going astray. And thus, even the feeble light of natural reason may render good service.

A Christian philosophy will regard it as its noblest task to prepare the way for supernatural faith. This is the precise reason why Saint Thomas Aquinas was so deeply concerned with the problem of how to build a pure philosophy on the basis of natural reason. He knew well that this was the only way of finding some common ground with unbelieving thinkers. If the latter are willing to join us at least part of the way, they may perhaps subsequently allow themselves to be guided farther than they originally intended to go. From the point of view of Christian philosophy, there should then be no misgivings about a common effort. Adhering to the principle, "Examine everything, and retain the best," Christian philosophy is willing to learn from the Greeks and from the moderns and to appropriate for itself whatever can meet the test of its own standards of measurement. On the other hand, it can well afford to display generously what it itself has to offer and then leave to others the task of examination and selection.

Unbelievers have no good reason to distrust the findings of Christian philosophy on the grounds that it uses as a standard of measurement not only the ultimate truths of reason but also the truths of faith. No one prevents them from applying the criterion of reason in full stringency and from rejecting everything that does not measure up to it. They may also freely decide whether they want to go further and take into account those findings that have been gained with the aid of revelation. In this case they will accept the truths of faith not as "theses" (as do believers) but only as "hypotheses." But as to whether or not the conclusions at which both arrive are in accord with the truths of reason, there prevails again a standard of measurement which both sides have in common. Unbelieving thinkers may then calmly consider whether or not they find themselves able to make their own the synthesis which results for Christian philosophers from the two sources of reason and revelation. And unbelievers must judge for themselves whether by accepting this additional knowledge they may perhaps gain a deeper and more comprehensive understanding of that which is. They will not, at any rate, shrink back from such an attempt if they are really as unbiased as, according to their own conviction, genuine philosophers ought to be.

PART

II

At the Foot of the Cross

6

Juxta Crucem Tecum Stare

As Edith Stein prepared to take her perpetual vows during Holy Week in April 1938, she wrote this poem, "Juxta Crucem Tecum Stare" (I Stood with You Beneath the Cross), imagining herself standing with Jesus' mother Mary on Good Friday.

Today I stood with you beneath the cross,
And felt more clearly than I ever did
That you became our Mother only there.
Even an earthly mother faithfully
Seeks to fulfill the last will of her son.
But you became the handmaid of the Lord:
The life and being of the God made man
Was perfectly inscribed in your own life.
So you could take your own into your heart,
And with the lifeblood of your bitter pains
You purchased life anew for every soul.
You know us all, our wounds, our imperfections;

But you also know the celestial radiance
Which your Son's love would shed on us in heaven.
Thus carefully you guide our faltering footsteps,
No price too high for you to lead us to our goal.
But those whom you have chosen for companions
To stand with you around the eternal throne,
They here must stand with you beneath the cross,
And with the lifeblood of their own bitter pains
Must purchase heavenly glory for those souls
Whom God's own Son entrusted to their care.

7

The Meaning of the Cross

When Edith Stein made her monastic vows, she took the name Sister Teresa Benedicta of the Cross, adding the epithet in homage of the mystic Carmelite Saint John of the Cross. In her book The Science of the Cross, *she writes about the symbol of the cross and what it means for believers today.*

WHEN WE SPEAK of a science of the cross, this is not to be understood in the usual meaning of science; we are not dealing merely with a theory, that is, with a body of true or presumably true propositions. Neither are we dealing with a structure built of ideas laid out in reasoned steps. We are dealing with a well-recognized truth – a theology of the cross – but a living, real, and effective truth. It is buried in the soul like a seed that takes root there and grows, making a distinct impression on the soul, determining what it does and omits, and by shining outwardly is recognized in this very doing and omitting. In this sense, as one speaks of a science of the saints, we speak of a science of the cross. From this living form and strength in one's innermost depths, a perspective of life arises, the image one has of God and of the world, and therefore one can find expression for it in a mode of thinking, in a theory. . . .

Frequently there is an excessive interior preoccupation with one's own personal concerns that refuses to attend to anything else. We know our interior rigidity is inappropriate and it pains us; knowing that it arises from a psychological law does not help us to overcome it. On the other hand, we rejoice when we can convince ourselves through experience that we are still able to feel deep, genuine joy; deep, genuine pain also seems to us a grace when compared to our rigid insensitivity.

This numbness of feeling is particularly painful for us in the religious sphere. Many believers are depressed because the facts of salvation history do not at all (or no longer) impress them as they ought, and lack the strong influence on their lives that they should exert. The example of the saints demonstrates to them how things should actually be: where there is genuine, lively faith, there the doctrine of faith and the tremendous deeds of God are the content of life. All else steps aside for it and is determined by it. This is holy realism, the original inner receptivity of depth, and finds in the soul a living, mobile, docile energy that allows itself to be easily and joyfully led and molded by that which it has received, unhampered by any mistaken inhibitions and rigidity. Such realism, when it leads a holy soul to accept the truths of faith, becomes the *science of the saints*. If the mystery of the cross becomes its *inner form*, it turns into a *science of the cross*.

THE SAVIOR HIMSELF spoke of the cross on various occasions and in varying senses. When he foretold his Passion and his death, he had before his eyes in the literal sense the shameful wood of the cross upon which he was to end his life. But when he said, "Whoever does not take up his cross and follow me is not worthy of me" (Matt. 10:38), or, "If anyone wishes to follow me, let him deny himself, take up his cross, and follow me" (Matt. 16:24), then is the cross the symbol of all that is difficult and oppressive and so against human nature that taking it upon oneself is like a journey to death. And the disciple of Jesus is to take up this burden daily.

The announcement of his death set the image of the Crucified One before his disciples, and even today sets it before one who reads or hears the gospel. Therein lies a silent challenge to respond appropriately. The appeals to follow on the way of the cross of life present that appropriate response and at the same time give an insight into the meaning of death on the cross. For upon the words of invitation there follows immediately the admonition: "Whoever wishes to save his life will lose it, but whoever loses his life for my sake will save it" (Matt. 16:25). Christ gives up his life in order to open the way to eternal life for humanity. However, to win eternal life, they too must give up their earthly life. They must die with Christ in order to rise with him: the lifelong death of suffering and of daily self-denial, and even, if necessary, the bloody death of a martyr for the gospel of Christ.

SOULS UNITED WITH CHRIST live out of his life – however, only in surrender to the Crucified when they have traveled the entire way of the cross with him. Nowhere is this expressed more clearly and more urgently than in the message of Saint Paul, who already had a well-developed science of the cross, a theology of the cross derived from inner experience:

> Christ sent me . . . to preach the gospel, and not with eloquent wisdom, lest the cross be emptied of its power. For the word of the cross is folly to those who are perishing, but to us who are being saved it is the power of God. . . . Jews demand signs and Greeks seek

> wisdom, but we preach Christ crucified, a stumbling block to Jews and folly to Gentiles, but to those who are called, both Jews and Greeks, Christ the power of God and the wisdom of God. For the foolishness of God is wiser than men, and the weakness of God is stronger than men." (1 Cor. 1:17–18, 22–25)

The *word from the cross* is the gospel of Paul – the message he announced to Jews and pagans. It is a plain witness, without a trace of grandiloquence, without any effort to convince on the grounds of reason. It derives its entire force from that which it proclaims. And that is the cross of Christ, that is, the death of Christ on the cross, and the crucified Christ himself. Christ is God's power and God's wisdom not only as one sent by God, as God's Son who is himself God, but as the Crucified One. For his death on the cross is the salvific solution invented by God's unfathomable wisdom. In order to show that human power and human wisdom are incapable of achieving salvation, he gives salvific power to what appears to human estimation to be weak and foolish, to him who wishes to be nothing on his own but allows the power of God alone to work in him, who has "emptied himself" and "become obedient to death on the cross" (Phil. 2:7–8).

The saving power: this is the power that awakens to life those in whom divine life had died through sin. This saving power has entered the *word from the cross* and through this word passes over into all who receive it, who open themselves to it, without demanding miraculous signs or human wisdom's reasons. In them it becomes the life-giving and life-forming power that we have named the science of the cross.

Paul brought it to fulfillment in himself: "Through the law, I died to the law, that I might live to God. I have been crucified with Christ; it is no longer I who live but Christ who lives in me; and the life that I now live in the flesh I live by faith in the Son of God who loved me and gave himself for me" (Gal 2:19–20). In those days when all turned into night around him but light filled his soul, the zealot for the law realized that the law was but the tutor on the way to Christ.

The law could prepare one to receive life, but of itself it could not give life. Christ took the yoke of the law upon himself in that he fulfilled it perfectly and died for and through the law. Just so did he free from the law those who wished to receive life from him. But they can receive it only if they relinquish their own life. For those who are baptized in Christ are baptized in his death. They are submerged in his life in order to become members of his body and, as such, to suffer and to die with him but also to arise with him to eternal, divine life. This life will be ours in its fullness only on the day of glory.

But even now we have – "in the flesh" – a share therein insofar as we *believe*: believe that Christ died for us in order to give us life. It is this faith that unites us to him as the members of a body are joined to the head, and opens for us the stream of his life. And so faith in the Crucified – a living faith joined to loving surrender – is for us entrance into life and the beginning of future glory. The cross, therefore, is our only claim to glory: "Far be it from me to glory except in the cross of our Lord Jesus Christ, by which the world has been crucified to me, and I to the world" (Gal. 6:14). He who has decided for Christ is dead to the world and the world to him. He carries in his body the marks of the Lord's wounds, is weak and despised by the people but is precisely therefore strong because the power of God is mighty in the weak.

Knowing this, Jesus' disciple not only takes up the cross that is laid upon him, but also crucifies himself: "Those who belong to Christ Jesus have crucified the flesh with its passions and desires" (Gal 5:24). They have waged an unrelenting battle against their nature, that the life of sin might die in them and room be made for the life of the spirit. That last is what is important. The cross has no purpose of itself. It rises on high and points above. But it is not merely a sign – it is Christ's powerful weapon; the shepherd's staff with which the divine David moves against the hellish Goliath; with it he strikes mightily against heaven's gate and throws it wide open. Then streams of divine light flow forth and enfold all who are followers of the Crucified.

8

Signum Crucis

For Edith Stein, the cross is the essential symbol of Christianity. She wrote this poem, "Signum Crucis" (Sign of the Cross), on November 16, 1937, about five months before she took her final vows.

Juxta crucem tecum stare!
These words you wrote in a little book
For someone who carries the sign of the cross.
With the shadow of the cross already cast over you,
It lowered onto your shoulder,
Hard and heavy.

Becoming human for the sake of humanity,
He gave the fullness of his human life
For the souls of his beloved.
He who individually formed each human heart,
In a new name he wants to reveal
The secret meaning of his being,
Which only he understands, which is his alone:

A Sure Way

He has united himself with each of his beloved
In his own, deeply mysterious way.
He gifts us from his human life
The fullness of the cross.

What is the cross?
It is the sign of the deepest indignity.
Whoever touches it is cast out of the human race.
Those who once cheered for him
Timidly turn away and know him no more.
Defenseless, he is helpless before his enemies.
Nothing remains for him on earth
But pain, torment, and death.

What is the cross?
It is the sign that points to heaven.
It rises high above earthly dust and fog
and into the pure light.
Let go of things that can be taken away.
Open your hands and cling to the cross:
It will carry you up into eternal light.

Look to the cross:
It spreads its beams,
Just as he opens his arms
As if to embrace the whole world:

Signum Crucis

Come here, all you weary and heavy laden.
Even you who called me: go to the cross with him.
It is the image of the God who died on the cross.
It ascends from earth to heaven
Like him who ascended to heaven,
And I would like to take it all with me.
Embrace the cross and you will have him,
The Truth, the Way, and the Life.
If you carry your cross, it will carry you,
And will bring you salvation.

9

The Dark Night of the Soul

In another selection from The Science of the Cross, *Edith Stein reflects on the meaning of night in the writings of Saint John of the Cross.*

NIGHT IS SOMETHING NATURAL: the counterpart of light, wrapping itself around us and all things. It is not an object in the actual, literal sense: night is invisible and formless. But still we perceive it, indeed it is nearer to us than all things and forms; it is more closely bound to our being. Just as light allows things to step forward with their visible qualities, so night devours them and threatens to devour us also. Whatever sinks into it is not simply nothing; it continues to exist but as indeterminate, invisible, and formless as night itself or shadowy, ghostlike, and therefore threatening.

Moreover, not only is our own being threatened through external dangers hidden by the night, but it is shocked interiorly by night itself. It robs us of the use of our senses, limits our movements, makes lame our strengths, banishes us to loneliness, makes us shadowy and ghostly ourselves. It is like a foretaste of death. And all this has not merely a vital, but a psychic-spiritual significance as well. The cosmic night affects us similarly to what in a figurative sense is called night. Or, turned around, whatever brings forth in us effects similar to those of the cosmic night is, in a figurative sense, called night.

We must be clear that the cosmic night already has a double face. The dark and uncanny night is other than the moonlit magic night, which is flooded by a mild, soft light. This softly lit night does not devour things but, instead, gives them a glowing nocturnal visage. Everything harsh, sharp, and glaring is muted and soothed, and characteristic traits are revealed that never appear in bright daylight. Voices can be heard that are drowned out by daytime noises. And not only does the light-filled night have its own values, but so does the dark one. The latter puts an end to the haste and noise of the day; it brings rest and peace. All of this pertains as well to what is referred to as psychic-spiritual. There is a night-like, gentle lucidity of the spirit, in which, freed from the drudgery of the day's duties, relaxed and recollected at the same time, it is absorbed in the profound relationships of its own being and life, of the world, and the world beyond. And there is a deep, grateful repose in the peace of night.

THE MYSTIC'S NIGHT is not to be understood in a cosmic sense. It does not impose itself on us from without but rather has its origin in the interior of the soul and affects only this single soul in whom it arises. The effects it produces, however, in the interior can be compared to those of the cosmic night: it entails a submersion of the exterior world even though outside it is bathed in bright daylight. It casts the soul into loneliness, desolation, and emptiness, stops the activity of all her faculties, frightens her by threatening horrors it conceals within itself. However, here there is also a nocturnal light that reveals a new world deep in the interior and at the same time illumines the outer world from within so that this outer is given back to us as entirely transformed.

SOMETHING ENTIRELY NEW is begun when the *dark night* starts. The entirely comfortable being-at-home in the world, the satiety of pleasures that it offers, the demand for these pleasures and the matter-of-course consent to these demands – all of this that human nature considers bright daily life – all of this is darkness in God's eyes and incompatible with the divine light. It has to be totally uprooted if room for God is to be made in the soul. Meeting this demand means engaging in battle with one's own nature all along the line, taking up one's cross and delivering oneself up to be crucified. Saint John of the Cross here invokes the Lord's saying in this connection: "Whoever does not renounce all that the will possesses cannot be my disciple" (cf. Luke 14:33).

That the domination of desires is truly darkness in the soul is demonstrated in full: the appetites weary and torment the soul, darken, besmirch, and weaken her, rob her of the Spirit of God because she turns away from him by her surrender to the animal spirit. To take up the battle against it, or to take one's cross upon oneself, means entering into the dark night actively. . . .

Active entry into the dark night of the senses is synonymous with ready willingness to take up the cross, and with persistence in carrying the cross. But one does not die from carrying the cross. And in order to pass completely through the night, a person must die to sin. One can deliver oneself up to crucifixion, but one cannot crucify oneself. Therefore that which the active night has begun must be completed by the passive night, that is, through God himself. Saint John writes: "No matter how much individuals do through their own efforts, they cannot actively purify themselves enough to be disposed in the least degree for the divine union of the perfection of love. God must take over and purge them in that fire that is dark for them."[1]

IT IS NO EXAGGERATION when we call the suffering of the souls in this state a crucifixion. In their inability to make use of their own faculties they are as though nailed fast. And to the dryness is added the torment of fear that they are on the wrong path. . . .

Were they to remain peacefully surrendered to this dark contemplation, they would soon experience inflaming love. "For contemplation is nothing else than a secret and peaceful and loving inflow of God, which, if not hampered, fires the soul in the spirit of love."[2]

In the beginning, this inflaming love is not commonly perceived. The soul feels rather only dryness and emptiness, sorrowful fear and concern. And if she does feel any of the love, it is as a painful yearning for God, a smarting wound of love. Only later will she recognize that God has purified her through the night of the senses and wishes to make the senses subject to the

1 John of the Cross, *The Dark Night*, 3.3

2 John of the Cross, *The Dark Night*, 1.10.6.

spirit. Then she will exclaim, "Oh, happy fate!" And she will clearly see what gain the "unnoticed escape" means for her: it has freed her from the servitude in which the senses had kept her, and little by little she is detached from all creatures and attracted to eternal goods. The *night of the senses* was for her the *narrow gate* that leads to life (Matt. 7:14).

Now she is to travel on the constricted road, which is the night of the spirit. Of course, few will come so far, yet the advantages of the first night are very great: the soul is granted self-knowledge; she gains insight into her own misery, no longer finds anything good in herself, and learns therefore to approach God with greater reverence. Yes, only now is she aware of the grandeur and majesty of God. Precisely this being freed from all sensory supports enables her to receive illumination and become receptive to the truth. . . .

In dryness and emptiness the soul becomes humble. The earlier arrogance disappears when one no longer finds in oneself anything that would give reason to look down on others; instead, others now appear to one to be more perfect, and love and esteem for them awakens in the heart. One is too occupied with one's own misery to be concerned about others. Through her helplessness the soul also becomes subservient and obedient; she longs for instruction in order to reach the right way. Spiritual avarice is thoroughly healed; when one no longer finds any practice to one's taste, one becomes very moderate and does whatever one does purely for the sake of God, without seeking any satisfaction for the self. And so it goes with all imperfections. All the confusion and unrest disappear with them. Instead, a deep peace and a constant remembrance of God are established. The only care that remains is the concern not to displease God.

The dark night becomes the school of all virtues: it exercises one in surrender and patience if one remains faithful in the spiritual life without seeking consolation or refreshment. The soul attains a pure love of God, so that all is done now only for God's sake. Perseverance despite all unpleasantness gives the soul strength and courage. Being completely purged of all sensory inclinations and appetites leads to a freedom of the spirit in which the twelve fruits of the spirit ripen. It gives security against the three enemies: the devil, the world, and the flesh.

10

The Night of Faith

In The Science of the Cross, *Edith Stein describes faith as darkness, since it requires trusting blindly in what one cannot see. But one must pass this way to reach the true light.*

DETACHMENT IS DESIGNATED as a night through which the soul must pass. It is this in a threefold sense: in regard to the *point of departure*, the *path*, and the *goal*. The point of departure is the desire for the things of this world, which the soul must renounce. But this renunciation transplants her into darkness, as though into nothingness. That is why it is called night. The world that we perceive with the senses is, after all, naturally the firm foundation that supports us, the house in which we feel at home, that nourishes us and provides us with everything necessary, the source of all our joys and gratifications. If this world is taken from us, or if we are forced to withdraw ourselves from it, it is truly as though the ground were swept away from under our feet and as though it became night all around us; as though we ourselves must sink and vanish.

But this is not so. In fact, we are set upon a surer way, albeit a dark way, one engulfed by night, the way of faith. It is a *way*, for it leads to the goal of union. But it is a nocturnal way, since in comparison to the clear insight of the natural understanding, faith is a dark knowledge: it acquaints us with something, but we do not get to see it.

That is why it must be said that the *goal* we reach on the way of faith is also night. God remains hidden from us on earth, even in the bliss of union. The eyes of the spirit are not adapted to the excessive radiance of his light, and gaze as it were into the darkness of night. But just as the cosmic night is not equally dark for its entire duration, the mystic night has its divisions of time and corresponding intensities. The submersion of the world of the senses is like the oncoming of night, when a mere twilight remains of the day's brightness. Faith, on the contrary, is the midnight darkness because here not only are the senses inactive but the knowledge from natural understanding is eliminated. The dawn of the new day of eternity, however, breaks into her night when the soul finds God.

IF ONE SPEAKS to others about something they have never seen, and if they know of nothing similar which could give them a clue, they may perhaps be able to accept the name, but they will never be able to form an image of the thing, as, for example, a person born blind will have no idea of color. Such is faith to the soul. It informs us of things we have never seen nor heard; nor do we know anything that might be similar to them. We can only accept what we are told by turning off the light of our natural knowledge. We have to agree with what we hear without having any of the senses elucidate it for us. Therefore, faith is a totally dark night for the soul. But it is precisely by these means that it brings her light: a knowledge of perfect certainty that exceeds all other knowledge and science so that one can arrive in perfect contemplation at a correct conception of faith.

From what was last said, it has not only been made clear that faith is a dark night, but also that it is a *way*: the way to the goal toward which the soul strives, to union with God. For it alone gives knowledge of God. And how is one to arrive at union with God without knowing him? However, in order to be led by faith to the goal, the soul must conduct itself in the right manner. She must enter into the night of faith of her own choice and by her own power. After having renounced all desire for creatures in the night of the senses, in order to reach God, she must now die to her natural faculties, her senses, and to her intellect also. For in order to reach the supernatural transformation, she must leave behind everything natural. Yes, she must divest herself, as well, of all supernatural goods when God grants her any of these. She must let go of everything that falls into the realm of her power of comprehension. "And she must remain in the dark like a blind man, leaning upon dark faith and choosing it as light and guide and not supporting herself by anything she understands or enjoys or feels or imagines. For all this is darkness that will lead her into error or delay. Faith, on the other hand, is above all such understanding, enjoyment, feeling, or imagining."[3] . . .

The soul must become totally blind to all of this and remain so in order to reach what faith teaches. For those who are not yet totally blind are reluctant to allow a guide to lead them; instead, they still depend on that which they can see themselves. . . . Should she support herself by her own faculties, the soul prepares only difficulties and obstacles for herself. To reach her goal, leaving her own path is synonymous with entering on the right path. . . .

3 John of the Cross, *Ascent*, 2.4.2.

She must elevate herself above all that is naturally and spiritually intelligible, above all she is able to understand and know in a natural way, as well as above all that is spiritual which one can taste and feel with the senses in this life. The more she still esteems all this the more she distances herself from the highest good. But if she considers all as slight in comparison to the highest good, she "will approach union swiftly by means of faith, which is also dark."[4] . . .

The divine light, then, already dwells in the soul by nature. But only when for God's sake she divests herself of all that is not God – that is what is called love! – will the soul be illumined by and transformed in God.

4 John of the Cross, Ascent, 2.4.5f.

PART III

Light Breaks In

II

Easter Morning

Written on April 20, 1924, just two years after her baptism and almost a decade prior to her entrance into the monastery, this poem is an early example of Edith Stein's religious poetry and one of the few poems of hers that celebrate the Resurrection.

Dark is the night of the grave,
but the radiance of the holy wounds
breaks through the heaviness of the stone,
lifts it lightly and suspended aside;
from the darkness of the tomb rises high
the transfigured, bright and radiant
newly risen body of the Son of Man.

Quietly he steps out of the cave
into the still, quiet morning twilight.
A light mist covers the earth;
it is now deeply illuminated

by a white gleam—
and the Savior walks through the silence
of the newly awakened earth.

Under his holy footsteps
bloom bright flowers, a new creation—
Where his robe softly brushes the ground,
an emerald gleam shines in the meadow.
From his hands his blessing flows
over the field and meadow in full, clear streams—
and in the morning dew of the fullness of grace
nature rejoices radiantly in the Risen One
as he walks silently toward his people.

12

The Mystery of Sacrifice

In this Christmas reflection, first delivered as a talk in 1931 shortly after leaving her post at a convent school in Speyer, Edith Stein contemplates what it means to be a Christian – to go the whole way with Jesus from the manger to the cross.

"THY WILL BE DONE," in its full extent, must be the guideline for the Christian life. It must regulate the day from morning to evening, the course of the year and the entire life. Only then will it be the sole concern of the Christian. All other concerns the Lord takes over. This one alone, however, remains ours as long as we live. Actually, it is a fact that we are not absolutely assured that we will always remain on the pathways of God. Just as the first human beings could fall from being children of God to strangers of God, so each of us hovers constantly on the cutting rim between the void and the fullness of divine life. And, sooner or later, we begin to realize this. In the childhood of the spiritual life, when we have just begun to allow ourselves to be directed by God, we feel his guiding hand quite firmly and surely. But it doesn't always stay that way. Whoever belongs to Christ must go the whole way with him. We must mature to adulthood; we must one day or another walk the way of the cross to Gethsemane and Golgotha. And all external sufferings are as nothing in comparison with the dark night of the soul, when the divine light no longer shines and the voice of the Lord no longer speaks. God is there, but he is hidden and silent. Why is that? Those are the divine secrets about which we are speaking, and these cannot be completely penetrated. Nevertheless, we can get a little insight. God became man so that we would once more share in his life. With that it begins, and that is its final goal.

But in between there is yet something else. Christ is God and man, and whoever wants to share his life must participate in his divine and human life. The human nature which he accepted gave him the possibility to suffer and to die. The divine nature that he possessed from all eternity gave value and redemptive power to his sufferings and death, which are continued in his mystical body and in each one of his members. To suffer and to die is the lot of every human being. But if we are living members of the body of Christ, then our own suffering and death receive redemptive power through the divinity of the Head. That is the objective reason why all the saints asked for suffering. It was not a morbid desire for suffering. From the viewpoint of human understanding, it may even appear to be perversion. Yet in the light of the redemptive mystery, it turns out to make the most common sense. Thus, even in the dark night of personal distance from God and abandonment, the one who is allied with God will stick it out firm as a rock. Perhaps divine foresight will take up his torment in order to free him from his personal enslavement. Therefore – "Thy will be done!" – also and even in the darkest night.

BUT CAN WE STILL SAY "Thy will be done" when we are no longer certain what God's will would have of us? Do we still have the means to hold to his ways when the inner light dies out? There are such means, indeed such strong means, that it really becomes virtually impossible to deviate on any matter of principle. God came to redeem us, to unite us with himself, with one another, and to conform our will to his. He knows our nature; he takes it into consideration and therefore he has given us everything that can help us to reach our goal.

The divine Child has become Teacher and has told us what we should do. In order to allow an entire human existence to be pervaded with divine life, it is not enough to kneel down once a year in front of the manger and allow oneself to be taken in by the spell of the Holy Night. One must be actively engaged with God one's entire life long, listen to the words that he spoke, which have been handed down to us, and then comply with these words. Above all, one must pray as the Savior himself has taught and so insistently emphasized again and again. "Ask and you shall receive." That is the sure promise of a hearing. And whoever prays from his heart his daily "Lord, thy will be done" may certainly be confident that he has not failed to meet the divine will, even where he is no longer even sure of himself.

Furthermore, Christ has not left us orphans. He sent his Spirit to teach us all truth; he founded his church, which is led by his Spirit, and has incorporated in her his representatives through whom his Spirit speaks to us in human language. In her he has united the faithful into a community and desires each one to be responsible for the other. Thus we are not alone, and wherever one cannot rely upon one's own judgment and even upon one's own prayer, it is there that the power of obedience and the power of intercession help.

"And the Word became flesh." That truth became a reality in the manger at Bethlehem. But it was to be fulfilled in yet another form: "Whoever eats my flesh and drinks my blood has eternal life." The Savior, who knows that we are human beings and will remain human beings who have to struggle daily with weaknesses, comes to our assistance in a truly divine manner. Just as the human body needs daily bread, so also does the divine life in us require constant nourishment. "This is the living bread which came down from heaven." Whoever really takes this as daily bread experiences each day the mystery of Christmas, the Word made flesh. And that is doubtless the surest way to maintain constant union with God, to grow each day more firmly and deeply into the mystical body of Christ. I am well aware that for many that is an all-too-radical request. In a practical sense, it will mean for most – when they first start – a complete change in their external and internal life. But that's exactly what it is supposed to be! To make room in our life for the eucharistic Lord, so that he can change our life into his, is that asking too much? One has time for so many useless things: all sorts of stupid stuff gathered from books, newspapers, and magazines; sitting around in bars and gabbling on the street for a half hour; all these are diversions which waste time and energy like crumbs. As a challenge to the whole day, should it not be possible to put aside a morning hour in which one is not distracted but recollected, in which energy is not wasted but gained?

But, of course, this requires more than just one hour. From one such hour to the next, one must so live that it may come again. It is no longer possible to "let yourself go," even if only for a time. You cannot escape the judgment of those with whom you associate daily. Even if no word is spoken, you sense how the others feel toward you. You may try to adapt yourself to your companions, and if it is not possible, your common life becomes a torture. It's the same in our daily encounter with the Lord. One becomes more and more sensitive to that which pleases him or not. If, on the whole, you were previously quite satisfied with yourself, it will now take a different turn. You will find much that is bad and change it if possible. And you will discover many things you cannot consider well and good, but which are nevertheless hard to change. Then gradually, you will become very small and humble: you will grow patient and indulgent toward the splinter in strange eyes because the beam in your own is brought into being; and finally, you will also learn to be patient with yourself in the inexorable light of the divine presence and to surrender yourself to the divine mercy which can take care of all that ridicules our energy. The road is long from the smugness of a "good Catholic" who "does his duty," reads a "good newspaper," "does the right thing," etc., but on the other hand does what he pleases, to a life in God's hand, in the simplicity of a child and the meekness of the tax collector. But whoever has once walked it will not go back again.

Being a child of God implies becoming little and grown-up at the same time. To live in accord with the Eucharist means to let go of one's own body voluntarily and to grow into the broad expanse of life in Christ. Those who seek the Lord within don't always desire to have their attention upon themselves and their own affairs. They will begin to take an interest in the concerns of the Lord. Participation in the daily Sacrifice automatically draws us into the liturgical life. The prayers and sacred rites of the altar service present the history of salvation to us again and again and allow us an ever-deeper insight into its meaning. The act of Sacrifice constantly impresses upon us the central mystery of our faith, the crucial point of world history, the mystery of the Incarnation and Sacrifice. Who could be present at the Holy Sacrifice with receptive mind and heart without being caught up by the very manner of the Sacrifice, without being taken in by the request that we ourselves and our puny personal lives rise up in the great work of the Redeemer?

The mysteries of Christianity are an inseparable whole. If you become absorbed in one of them, you are drawn to all the others. Thus the road from Bethlehem leads irresistibly to Golgotha, from the manger to the cross. When the most holy Virgin carried the Child to the temple, she heard the prophecy that a sword would pierce her soul, that this Child was destined for the rise and fall of many as a sign of contradiction. It is the announcement of the Passion, of the struggle between light and darkness that was already present at the manger.

In many years, Candlemas and Septuagesima occur almost simultaneously: the celebration of the Incarnation and the preparation for the Passion. The star of Bethlehem shines forth in the dark night of sin. Upon the radiance that goes forth from the manger, there falls the shadow of the cross. In the dark of Good Friday, the light is extinguished, but it rises more brightly as the sun of grace on the morning of the Resurrection. The road of the Incarnate Son of God is through the cross and suffering to the splendor of the Resurrection. To arrive with the Son of Man through suffering and death at this splendor of the Resurrection is the road for each one of us, for all humankind.

13

The Holy Face

Written on December 5, 1937, for the second Sunday of Advent, this poem contemplates the image of Jesus' face, which reveals both his humanity and his divinity.

You who loved
As no one has ever loved,
At the end of your earthly life
You gave us the comfort and consolation
That you longed to be with us until the end of time.

Now you dwell hidden among us.
At all times and in all places,
Comfort, light, and strength
Stream down from your tent into the souls
That seek refuge in your presence.
They look lovingly up to the little host,
The quiet image of purity and peace.

In the hearts of those who love you
The desire to see you in the flesh never fades;

A Sure Way

You, the most beautiful of all children
In your human form.
In a never-ending effort, the artistic spirit
Renders image after image:
The child of God in his mother's arms,
The little boy in the circle of scribes,
The Master teaching amidst his disciples,
The Man of Sorrows on the cross in agony.
But no image of man gives us
You.

The time came, when the power of darkness
Wrenched faith from our hearts,
The embers of love grew cold.
Ever smaller became the faithful flock,
And your dwellings became deserted.
And as of late,
As faith, hope, and love have dwindled,
You unveiled your holy face,
The face of the one who suffered on the cross
And who closed his eyes in the sleep of death.

As if from behind a veil, we witness suffering
In these holy, sublime features.
So great, so beyond measure is this suffering,
That we cannot grasp and comprehend it.

But you suffered in silence,
And a power was in you
That subdued excessive suffering.
You were its Lord when you surrendered yourself to it.
A deep peace
Flows from these features
And speaks:
It is done.

The one you bind to you forever,
You cast the mysterious veil over her:
She suffers your suffering with you
And suffers like you,
Hidden, quietly and deeply at peace.

14

The Hidden Life and Epiphany

Stein wrote this message to the sisters in her religious order for the Feast of Epiphany, 1940, while cloistered at Echt, the Netherlands. The hidden stirring of the Holy Spirit in human hearts sometimes leads to great epiphanies but often bears fruit that goes unheralded.

WHEN THE GENTLE LIGHT of the Advent candles begins to shine in the dark days of December – a mysterious light in a mysterious darkness – it awakens in us the consoling thought that the divine light, the Holy Spirit, has never ceased to illumine the darkness of the fallen world. He has remained faithful to his creation, regardless of all the infidelity of creatures. And if the darkness would not allow itself to be penetrated by the heavenly light, there were nevertheless some places always predisposed for it to blaze.

A ray from this light fell into the hearts of our original parents even during the judgment to which they were subjected. This was an illuminating ray that awakened in them the knowledge of their guilt, an enkindling ray that made them burn with fiery remorse, purifying and cleansing, and made them sensitive to the gentle light of the star of hope which shone for them in the words of promise of the "protoevangelium," the original gospel (Gen. 3:15).

As were the hearts of the first human beings, so down through the ages again and again human hearts have been struck by the divine ray. Hidden from the whole world, it illuminated and irradiated them, let the hard, encrusted, misshapen matter of these hearts soften, and then with the tender hand of an artist formed them anew into the image of God. Seen by no human eye, this is how living building blocks were and are formed and brought together into a church that is invisible at first. However, the visible church grows out of this invisible one in ever new, divine deeds and revelations that shed their light – ever new *epiphanies*. The silent working of the Holy Spirit in the depths of the soul made the patriarchs into friends of God. However, when they came to the point of allowing themselves to be used as his pliant instruments, he established them in an external, visible efficacy as bearers of historical development, and awakened from among them his chosen people. Therefore

Moses, too, was educated quietly and then sent as the leader and lawgiver.

Not everyone whom God uses as an instrument must be prepared in this way. People may also be instruments of God without their knowledge and even against their will, possibly even people who neither externally nor interiorly belong to the church. They would then be used like the hammer or chisel of the artist, or like a knife with which the vinedresser prunes the vines. For those who belong to the church, outer membership can also temporally precede interior, and in fact can be materially significant for it (as when someone without faith is baptized and then comes to faith through the public life in the church). But it finally comes down to the interior life; formation moves from the inner to the outer. The deeper a soul is bound to God, the more completely surrendered to grace, the stronger will be its influence on the form of the church. Conversely, the more an era is engulfed in the night of sin and estrangement from God, the more it needs souls united to God. And God does not permit a deficiency. The greatest figures of prophecy and sanctity step forth out of the darkest night. But for the most part the formative stream of the mystical life remains invisible. Certainly, the decisive turning points in world history are substantially co-determined by souls whom no history book ever mentions. And we will only find out about those souls to whom we owe the decisive turning points in our personal lives on the day when all that is hidden is revealed.

Because hidden souls do not live in isolation, but are a part of the living nexus and have a position in a great divine order, we speak of an invisible church. Their impact and affinity can remain hidden from themselves and others for their entire earthly lives. But it is also possible for some of this to become visible in the external world. This is how it was with the persons and events intertwined in the mystery of the Incarnation. Mary and Joseph, Zechariah and Elizabeth, the shepherds and the kings, Simeon and Anna – all of these had behind them a solitary life with God and were prepared for their special tasks before they found themselves together in those awesome encounters and events and, in retrospect, could understand how the paths left behind had led to this climax. Their astounded adoration in the presence of these great deeds of God is expressed in the songs of praise that have come down to us.

In the people who are gathered around the manger, we have an analogy for the church and its development. Representatives of the old royal dynasties to whom the savior of the world was promised and representatives of faithful people constitute the relationship between the Old and the New Covenants. The kings from the faraway East indicate the Gentiles for whom salvation is to come from Judea. So here there is already "the church made up of Jews and Gentiles." The kings at the manger represent seekers from all lands and peoples. Grace led them before they ever belonged to the external church. There lived in them a pure longing for truth that did not stop at the boundaries of native doctrines and traditions. Because God is truth and because he wants to be found by those who seek him with their whole hearts, sooner or later the star had to appear to show these wise men the way to truth. And so they now stand before the Incarnate Truth, bow down and worship it, and place their crowns at its feet, because all the treasures of the world are but a little dust compared to it.

And the kings have a special meaning for us too. Even though we already belonged to the external church, an interior impulse nevertheless drove us out of the circle of inherited viewpoints and conventions. We knew God, but we felt that he desired to be sought and found by us in a new way. Therefore, we wanted to open ourselves and sought a star to show us the right way. And it arose for us in the grace of vocation. We followed it and found the divine infant. He stretched out his hands for our gifts. He wanted the pure *gold* of a heart detached from all earthly goods; the *myrrh* of a renunciation of all the happiness of this world in exchange for participation in the life and suffering of Jesus; the *frankincense* of a will that surrenders itself and strains upward to lose itself in the divine will. In return for these gifts, the divine child gave us himself.

But this admirable exchange was not a one-time event. It fills our entire lives. After the solemn hour of bridal surrender, there followed the everyday life of observance in the Order. We had to "return to our own country," but "taking another way" (Matt. 2:12), escorted by the new light that had blazed up for us at those solemn places. The new light commands us to search anew. "God lets himself be sought," says Saint Augustine, "to let himself be found. He lets himself be found to be sought again." After each great hour of grace, it is as if we were but beginning now to understand our vocation. Therefore, an interior need prompts us to renew our vows repeatedly. That we do so on the feast of the three kings, whose pilgrimage and affirmation are for us a symbol for our lives, has a deep meaning. To each authentic, heartfelt renewal of vows, the divine Child responds with renewed acceptance and a deeper union. And this means a new, hidden operation of grace in our souls. Perhaps it is revealed in an epiphany, the work of God becoming visible in our external behavior and the activity noticed by those around us. But perhaps it also bears fruit that, though observed, conceals from all eyes the mysterious source from which its vital juices pour.

Today we live again in a time that urgently needs to be renewed at the hidden springs of God-fearing souls. Many people, too, place their last hope in these hidden springs of salvation. This is a serious warning cry: Surrender without reservation to the Lord who has called us. This is required of us so that the face of the earth may be renewed. In faithful trust, we must abandon our souls to the sovereignty of the Holy Spirit. It is not necessary that we experience the epiphany in our lives. We may live in confident certainty that what the Spirit of God secretly effects in us bears its fruits in the kingdom of God. We will see them in eternity.

15

Holy Night

This poem, written on December 6, 1937, is dedicated to Edith Stein's sister, Rosa, in memory of her conversion to Christianity and baptism a year prior, on Christmas Eve 1936.

My Lord and God,
You have led me down a long, dark path,
Stony and hard,
Often my strength wanted to fail me,
I had lost all hope of ever seeing the light.
But when in the deepest pain my heart stopped,
A clear, gentle star appeared before me.
It led me faithfully—I followed it,
Tentatively at first, then ever more certain.
Until at last I stood at the gate of a church.
It opened—I asked for entrance.
Out of a priest's mouth your blessing greets me.
Inside, star after star falls into line.

A Sure Way

Red starry flowers show me the way to you.
They await you in the Holy Night.
But your goodness
Lets them light my path to you.
They lead me forward.
The secret that deep in my heart
I once had to hide,
Now I may proclaim boldly:
I believe—I have faith!
The priest leads me up the steps to the altar:
I bow my brow—
Holy water flows over my head.

Is it possible, Lord, to be born again,
When one is already middle-aged?
You said it and it became my reality.
The burden of a long life of guilt and suffering
Fell from me.
Upright I received the white cloak,
Which they laid around my shoulders,
The bright image of purity.
In my hands I carry a candle.
Its flame proclaims
That your holy life burns in me.

Holy Night

My heart has now become a creche
That awaits your arrival.

Not for long!
Mary, your mother as well as mine,
Has given me her name.
At midnight she lays her newborn child
Upon my breast.

O, the heart cannot comprehend
What you have prepared for those who love you.
Now I have you and I will never leave you.
Wherever the road of my life goes,
You are with me,
Nothing can ever separate me from your love.

16

The Summons of Christmas

Edith Stein reflects on the wondrous story of Jesus' birth and what it asks of us: to become one with God, to become one with others in God, and to extend God's love to all. This text is from the same 1931 talk as "The Mystery of Sacrifice" above.

WHEN THE DAYS grow shorter and shorter, when – in a normal winter – the first snowflakes fall, then, quietly and softly, thoughts of Christmas begin to surface, and from the mere word a certain magic exudes that affects every heart. Even those of other faiths or of no faith at all, to whom the story of the Child of Bethlehem has no meaning, prepare for the feast and make plans to convey its joy here or there. Months and weeks in advance, a warmth like a stream of love flows over the whole world. A festival of love and joy – that is the star which beckons all humankind in the first winter months.

For Christians, it is yet something more. The star leads them to the manger with the little Child who brings peace to the earth. In countless endearing pictures, artists have created the scene for our eyes; ancient legends, replete with all the magic of childhood, sing to us about it. Whoever lives along with the church hears the ancient chants and feels the longing of the spirit in the Advent hymns; and whoever is familiar with the inexhaustible fount of sacred liturgy is daily confronted by the great prophet of the Incarnation with his powerful words of warning and promise:

> *Drop down dew from above and let the clouds rain the Just One! The Lord is near! Let us adore him! Come, Lord, and do not delay! Jerusalem, rejoice with great joy, for your Savior comes to you!*[1]

From December 17 to 24, the great O Antiphons to the Magnificat call out with ever greater longing and fervor their "*Come, to set us free.*" And with still more promise (on the last Advent Sunday), "*Behold, all is fulfilled,*" then, finally, "*Today you shall know that the Lord is coming and tomorrow you shall see his splendor.*"

---

1 Isa. 45:8 and Zech. 9:9. Stein is working through the Advent liturgy *Rorate coeli*, here set in italic.

Yes, on that evening when the lights on the tree are lit and the gifts are being exchanged, that unfulfilled longing is still there groping for another ray of light until the bells for Midnight Mass ring out, and the miracle of the Holy Night is renewed upon altars bedecked with lights and flowers: "*And the Word was made flesh.*" Now the moment of blessed fulfillment has arrived.

Each of us has no doubt already experienced such Christmas bliss. Still, heaven and earth are not yet united. The star of Bethlehem remains a star in the dark night even today. On the day after Christmas the church removes her white garments and clothes herself in the color of blood, and on the fourth day in the violet of mourning: Stephen, the first martyr, the first to follow his Lord to death, and the infants of Bethlehem and Judea who were brutally slaughtered by crude henchmen, all have a place around the Child in the manger. What is the meaning of this message? Where now are the jubilant sounds of the heavenly choir? Where the peaceful bliss of Holy Night? Where is the peace on earth? Peace to those of good will; but not all are of good will. Therefore, the Son of the eternal Father must leave the splendor of heaven, because the mystery of evil has wrapped the earth in dark night.

Darkness covered the earth and he came as light to illumine the darkness, but the darkness did not comprehend him. To those who received him, he brought light and peace – peace with the Father in heaven, peace with everyone who, like them, are children of light and children of the heavenly Father, a deep interior peace of the heart – but not to the children of darkness. To them the Prince of Peace does not bring peace but the sword. He remains for them the stumbling block of scandal against which they charge and are smashed. That is the one hard and serious fact which we may not allow to be obscured by the visible attraction of the Child in the manger.

The mystery of the Incarnation and the mystery of evil belong together. The dark night of sin stands in stark and sinister contrast with the Light which came down from heaven. The Child in the manger extends his little hands, and his smile seems to be saying what would come forth later from the lips of the Man: "Come to me all you who are weary and heavy burdened"; and the poor shepherds out on the hills of Bethlehem, who heard the good news of the angel, follow his call and make their way with the simple answer, "Let us go to Bethlehem." Upon the kings from the Orient, who followed the wondrous star with similar simplicity, the Infant's hands also dropped the dew of grace, and "they rejoiced with great joy." These hands give and request at the same time: you wise men, lay down your wisdom and become like children; you kings, give up your crowns and your treasures and bow down meekly before the King of kings; do not hesitate to take up the burdens, sorrows, and weariness which his service demands. You children, who as yet cannot give of your own free will, of you these little hands will request your gentle life before it has even begun; it can serve no better purpose than sacrifice in praise of the Lord.

"Follow me," say the little hands, words which later would come from the lips of the Man. Thus they spoke to the disciple whom the Lord loved and who is now also part of the group at the manger. Saint John, the young man with the pure, youthful heart, followed without asking, "Where to? Why?" He left his father's boat and went with the Lord along all his ways, even to Golgotha. "Follow me" – young Stephen also understood this. He followed the Lord in the struggle against the powers of darkness, the blindness of obstinate unbelief; he bore witness to him with his word and his blood; he followed him in his spirit, the spirit of love, which resists sin but loves the sinner, and even in death intercedes with God on behalf of the murderer. These are the figures of light who kneel around the manger: the gentle, innocent children; the faithful shepherds, the humble kings; Stephen, the enthusiastic youth; and the beloved apostle, John – all of them followed the call of the Lord.

In contrast to them, there is the night of incomprehensible callousness and blindness: the scribes who have information as to the time and place where the Savior of the world is to be born, but who do not say, "Let us go to Bethlehem!"; and King Herod, who wants to kill the Lord of Life. In the presence of the Child in the manger, the spirits line up to take sides. He is the King of kings and Lord of life and death. He utters his "follow me," and whoever is not for him is against him. He also speaks for us and invites us to choose between light and darkness.

WHERE THAT WILL LEAD US on this earth we do not know and should not ask beforehand. We only know this: that for those who love the Lord, all things work out for good. And in addition, that the paths which the Lord directs lead out beyond this earth.

O wonderful exchange! The Creator of humankind, by taking on a human body, imparts to us his divinity. It is for this wondrous task that the Savior came into this world. God became a child of man so that the human race could become children of God. One of our race severed the bond of our divine adoption; one of us had to bind it up again and pay for the sin. No one from the ancient, sick, and degenerate race could do it. A new, healthy, and noble sprout had to be grafted. He became one of us; but even more than that, one with us. That is precisely the wonderful thing about the human race – that we are all one. If it were otherwise, were we all to exist as independent and separate individuals, then the fall of one could not have brought about the fall of all. Then, on the other hand, the price of sin could probably have been paid for us and charged to us, but his justification would not have passed on to sinners; no vindication would have been possible. But he came to be a mysterious body with us: he as head, we as members. Let us place our hands in the hands of the divine Child; let us speak our "yes" to his "follow me." Thus we shall be his and the path shall be open for his divine life to pass over upon us.

That is the beginning of eternal life in us. It is not yet a blessed vision of God in the light of glory. It is still the darkness of faith, but it is no longer of this world; it is already a stance in the kingdom of God. When the ever-blessed Virgin spoke her "Let it be done," it was the beginning of the kingdom of God on earth, and she was the first handmaid. And all who recognized the Child in word and deed before and after his birth – Saint Joseph, Saint Elizabeth with her child, and all those standing around the manger – entered into the kingdom of God. Things turned out differently than people had imagined according to the psalms and the prophets. The Romans remained the rulers of the land and the high priests and scribes continued to keep the poor people under their yoke. Those who followed the Lord carried their heavenly treasure invisibly within themselves. Their temporal burdens were not removed; on the contrary, many others were added. Yet they bore within themselves an exhilarating strength which softened the yoke and lightened the burden. This remains true today for every child of God. The divine life which is enkindled in the soul is the Light that came into the darkness – the mystery of the Holy Night. Those who bear it within themselves understand its meaning. For others, on the contrary, it remains an enigma regardless of any explanation. The entire Gospel of John concerning the eternal Light which is love and life deals with it. God is in us and we in him; that is our portion of the kingdom of God, established by the Incarnation.

ONENESS WITH GOD: that is the first sign. However, a second proceeds from this. If Christ is the head and we the members in the mystical body, then we relate to each other as member to member and we are all one in God, a divine life. If God is in us and if he is love, then it cannot be otherwise but that we love one another. Therefore, our love for our brothers and sisters is the measure of our love for God. But it is different from a natural, human love that affects this one or that one who may be related to us, or who may be close to us because of the bonds of temperament or common interests. The rest are "strangers" who don't concern us, or perhaps even annoy us by their presence, so that love is kept as far away as possible. For the Christian there is no "strange human being." The person next to us, the one who needs us most, is in every instance our "neighbor." It makes no difference whether he is related to us or not, whether we "like" him or not, whether he is "morally worthy" of help or not. The love of Christ knows no bounds, never ceases, and never retreats in the face of hatred or foul play. He came for the sake of sinners and not for the righteous. If the love of Christ lives in us, then we do as he did and seek after the lost sheep.

Natural love seeks to possess the beloved entirely and, as far as possible, exclusively. Christ came to win back lost humankind for the Father; those who love with Christ's love will want people for God and not for themselves. Of course, this is the surest way to possess them forever; for whenever we have entrusted a person to God, we are one with him in God, whereas the craving to overpower sooner or later always leads to loss. This is true for the other's soul as well as for one's own and for every external possession. Whoever is anxiously out to win and possess, loses; whoever hands over to God, wins.

WITH THAT WE TOUCH UPON a third sign of the child of God. To be one with God was the first; that all may be one in God, the second. The third: "By this do I know that you love me: if you keep my commandments" (John 14:15). To be a child of God means to go hand-in-hand with God; to do his will, not one's own; to place all one's hopes and cares in his hands and no longer be concerned about one's self or future. Thereupon rest the freedom and the good cheer of the child of God. Yet how few of the truly devout, or even those truly heroic and willing to make sacrifices, possess them. They always go around bowed down under the heavy burden of their worries and responsibilities. They are all familiar with the parable of the birds of the air and the lilies of the field. But whenever they encounter anyone who has no means, nor income, nor insurance and is nonetheless unconcerned about the future, they shake their head, completely baffled. Of course, those who expect that their heavenly Father will always see to it that they are well off and well taken care of could very well be greatly mistaken. Trust in God will remain unshakably firm only if it is willing to accept from the Father's hand anything and everything. He is the only one who knows what is good for us. And if sometimes need and want are more in order than a pleasantly comfortable living, or misfortune and humiliation rather than honor and prestige, we must be prepared for that as well. If we can do this, we will freely live for the present and for the future.

PART IV

Women's Spirituality

17

The Soul of Woman

Coming of age at the turn of the twentieth century, Edith Stein witnessed significant changes in society. Throughout her life, she was particularly attuned to questions of gender and the role of women. The following two readings are excerpted from "Spirituality of the Christian Woman," a talk she delivered in 1932, during her last year as a lecturer at a teachers' college in Münster.

CAN WE SPEAK in general terms of the soul of woman? Every human soul is unique; no one soul is the same as any other. How can we then speak of the soul in general? But even if we intend to disregard individualities, is there then one type of woman? Can the complete multiplicity which we meet with in life be reduced to a single unity?

I believe that, while there are types of women, we will always find fundamentally the compulsion to become what the woman's soul should be, the drive to allow the latent humanity, set in her precisely in its individual stamp, to ripen to the greatest possible perfect development. The deepest feminine yearning is to achieve a loving union which, in its development, validates this maturation and simultaneously stimulates and furthers the desire for perfection in others; this yearning can express itself in the most diverse forms, and some of these forms may appear distorted, even degenerate. Such yearning is an essential aspect of the eternal destiny of woman. It is not simply a human longing but is specifically feminine and distinct from the specifically masculine nature.

Man's essential desires reveal themselves in action, work, and objective achievements. He is less concerned with problems of being, whether his own or of others. Certainly being and doing cannot be wholly separated. The human soul is not a complete, static, unchanging, monolithic existence. It is being in the state of becoming and in the process of becoming; the soul must bring to fruition those predispositions with which it was endowed when coming into the world; however, it can develop them only through activation. Thus woman can achieve perfect development of her personality only by activating her spiritual powers. So do men, even without envisaging it as a goal, work in the same way when they endeavor to perform anything objectively. In both instances the structure of the soul is fundamentally the same. The soul is housed in a body on whose vigor and health its own vigor and health depend – even if not exclusively nor simply. On the other hand, the body receives its nature as body – life, motion, form, gestalt, and spiritual significance – through the soul. The world of the spirit is founded on sensuousness, which is spiritual as much as physical: the intellect, knowing its activity to be rational, reveals a world; the will intervenes creatively and formatively in this world; the emotions receive this world inwardly and put it to the test. But the extent and relationship of these powers vary from one individual to another, and particularly from man to woman.

THIS PRESENTS US with the task of investigating what the formative powers are through which woman's soul can be led to the nature for which it is intended and can be protected from the degeneration with which it is threatened. Each woman's particular spiritual disposition is the substance that must be formed: the basic faculties that exist originally are unique in degree and in kind to each human soul. It is not inanimate material that must be entirely developed or formed in an exterior way, as is clay by the artist's hand or stone by the weather's elemental forces; it is rather a living formative root that possesses within itself the driving power toward development in a particular direction; the seed must grow and ripen into the perfect gestalt, perfect creation. Thus envisaged, formation of the spirit is a developmental process similar to that of a plant. However, the plant's organic growth and development do not come about wholly from within: there are also exterior influences which work together to determine its formation, such as the climate and soil; in the same way, both interior and exterior factors play a role in the soul's formation. . . .

A woman has capabilities of caring, protecting, and promoting that which is coming into being and growing. She thereby has the gift to live in close physical contact and to compose herself in silence; on the other hand, she is created to endure pain, to adapt and abnegate herself. She is psychically directed to the concrete, the individual, and the personal: she has the ability to grasp the concrete in its individuality and to adapt herself to it, and she has the longing to help this peculiarity to its development. . . .

The woman who fulfills her natural destiny as wife and mother also has her duties for God's kingdom –

initially, the propagation of human beings destined for this kingdom, but then also works for the salvation of souls; only for her, this lies first within the family circle. On the other hand, even in the life which is wholly consecrated to God, there is also need for the development of natural forces, except that now they can be more exclusively dedicated to problems pertaining to the kingdom of God and can thereby even benefit a wider circle of people. These works for God's kingdom are not foreign to feminine nature but, on the contrary, are its highest fulfillment and also the highest conceivable enhancement of the human being. This is true as long as the action of personal relationship is born out of love for God and neighbor, works through love of God and neighbor, and leads to love of God and neighbor.

18

Male and Female in the Image of God

This chapter is taken from the same 1932 lecture as the previous chapter. Radical in its time, it considers how both femininity and masculinity can reflect the nature of God.

WOMAN'S DESTINY STEMS from eternity. She must be mindful of eternity to define her vocation in this world. If she complies with her vocation, she achieves her destiny in eternal life.

"God created man in his image; male and female he created them." When God put humanity into the world, not as a single but as a dual species, there had to be a different meaning of life for each sex in addition to a mutual one. Both were formed according to God's image. Each finite creature can reflect only a fraction of the divine nature; thus, in the diversity of his creatures, God's infinite unity and oneness appear to be broken into an effulgence of manifold rays. Just so, male and female imitate the divine prototype in different ways.

Augustine and Thomas and those following in their traditions find a likeness of the Trinity in the human spirit. Although perceived in many ways, it is accepted by most that the Father, Son, and Holy Spirit are rendered back in being, knowledge, and love. Divine wisdom was incarnated as person in the Son; love came as person in the Spirit. If the intellect is seen as predominant in masculine nature and the emotions in woman's nature, we can understand why a particular association is constantly being made between woman's nature and the Holy Spirit.

Inasmuch as the Holy Spirit is deity, we find it again in woman's destiny as "Mother of the Living." The Spirit goes out of itself and enters into the creature as the begetting and perfecting fruitfulness of God; just so does woman bring forth new life from her life and help her child to a most perfect development when he or she attains an autonomous existence. So do we also find the Holy Spirit in all works of womanly love and compassion, inasmuch as it is the Holy Spirit, as father of the poor, consoler and helper, who heals the wounded, warms the numb, refreshes the thirsty, and bestows all good gifts. In womanly purity and gentleness we find mirrored the spirit which cleanses the defiled and makes pliant the unbending; it abounds not only in those who may be already pure and gentle but also in those women who want to spread purity and gentleness around themselves. This "gracious spirit" wants nothing else than to be divine light streaming out as a serving love; nothing is more contrary to it than vanity that looks out for itself, and desire that wants to amass for itself. That is why the foremost sin of pride, in which vanity and desire coincide, is a falling-off from the spirit of love and a defection from feminine nature itself.

19

Women's Destiny

From her youthful activism to her professional career, Edith Stein was deeply invested in promoting the equality of all people as beloved children of God, with particular attention to the emancipation of women. This chapter is from her 1928 lecture "The Significance of Woman's Intrinsic Value in National Life."

IN WOMAN, THERE LIVES a natural drive toward *totality* and *self-containment*. This drive has a twofold direction: she herself would like to become a complete human being, one who is fully developed in every way; and she would like to help others to become so. . . .

The personal attitude is objectively justified and valuable because the human person is more precious than all objective values. All truth is discerned by persons; all beauty is beheld and measured by persons. All objective values exist in this sense for persons. And behind all things of value to be found in the world stands the *person of the Creator* who, as prefigurement, encloses all earthly values in himself and transmits them. In the area of our common experience, the human being is the highest among creation since our personality is created in the image of God. It is the whole person about whom we are speaking: that human being in whom God's image is developed most purely, in whom the gifts which the Creator has bestowed do not wither but bloom, and in whom the faculties are balanced in conformity to God's image and God's will – the will led by intellect, and the lower faculties bridled by intellect and will.

Each human being is called naturally to this total humanity, and the desire for it lives in each one of us. We may consider that the drive for this, which is particularly strong in woman, is well related to her particular destiny as companion and mother. To be a companion means to be a support and mainstay, and to be able to be so, a woman herself must stand firmly; however, this is possible only if inwardly everything is in right order and rests in equilibrium. To be a mother is to nourish and protect true humanity and bring it to development. But again, this necessitates that she possess true humanity herself, and that she is clear as to what it means; otherwise, she cannot lead others to it. Women can become suitable for this double duty if they have the correct personal attitude. Yet woman does not necessarily possess this by nature. The initial form of feminine singularity is primarily a degeneration and obstruction of this true attitude. On the one hand, it is a bias to secure her own personal importance, by which she may busy herself and others; also, it is an inability to endure criticism, which is experienced as an attack on her person. These yearnings for importance, yearnings toward unlimited recognition, are extended to everything unique to her person. Her own husband must be recognized as the very best husband, her own children must be known as the most beautiful, clever, and gifted. This is blind feminine love, which dulls realistic judgment and renders her completely unsuitable for the designated feminine vocation. Along with this excessive vindication of her own person goes an excessive interest in others, a perverse desire to meddle in others' personal lives, a passion for wanting to control people. Excess of interest in both her own and the stranger's personality merge in feminine surrender, the urge to lose herself completely in another human being; but in so doing, she does justice neither to herself nor to the humanity of another, and at the same time becomes unfit for exercising other duties. . . .

WHERE DO WE HAVE the concrete image of total humanity? God's image walked among us in human form in the Son of Man, Jesus Christ. If we reflect on how this image speaks to us in the simple account of the Gospels, it opens our eyes. The better we get to know the Savior, the more we are conquered by his sublimity and gentleness, by his kingly freedom which knows no other obligation than submission to the Father's will, and by his freedom from all living creatures, which is simultaneously the foundation for his compassionate love toward each living creature. And the deeper this image of God penetrates into us, the more it awakens our love. In this way, we become more sensitive to all falling away from him in ourselves and in others; our eyes are opened, free of all extenuations, to true knowledge of human nature. And if we lack the power to endure the sight of human weakness in ourselves and in others, only a look at the Savior is needed. Indeed, he has not turned from our misery in horror, but he came to us exactly because of this misery and took it upon himself. Thus, he himself has the remedy if we do not know where to find redress. Through his sacraments, he purifies and strengthens us. And if we turn confidently to him, which is his will, his spirit enters us and converts us; through union with him, we learn to dispense with human props and to gain the freedom and strength we need to be a support and mainstay for others. He himself guides us and shows us how we should guide others. We therefore achieve total humanity through him and, simultaneously, the right personal attitude. Whoever looks to him and is concentrated on him sees God, the archetype of all personality and the embodiment of all value. The surrender to which feminine nature inclines is here appropriate; on the other hand, we also find here the absolute love and surrender for which we seek vainly in people. And surrender to Christ does not make us blind and deaf to the needs of others. On the contrary, we now seek for God's image in each human being and want, above all, to help each human being win his or her freedom. Accordingly, we can say: the intrinsic value of woman consists essentially in exceptional receptivity for God's work in the soul, and this value comes to unalloyed development if we abandon ourselves confidently and unresistingly to this work.

Only now have we come to the second part of our theme: the significance of woman for national life. This significance presents itself as a simple conclusion from what has been said. What is, then, the great sickness of our time and people? There is an inner disunion, a complete deficiency of set convictions and strong principles, an aimless drifting. Therefore, the great mass of humanity seeks an anesthetic in ever new, ever more refined delights. Those who wish to maintain a sober level of life, in order to protect themselves from contemporary turmoil, frequently annihilate this level by one-sided professional work; but even they cannot do anything to escape the turmoil. Only whole human beings as we have described them are immune to the contemporary sickness: such beings are steadfast on eternal first principles, unperturbed in their views and in their actions by the changing modes of thoughts, follies, and depravities surrounding them. Every such individual is like a pillar to which many can fasten themselves, thereby attaining a firm footing. Consequently, when women themselves are once again whole persons and when they help others to become so, they create healthy, energetic spores supplying healthy energy to the entire national body.

FINALLY, WOMAN'S INTRINSIC VALUE can work in every place and thereby institute grace, completely independent of the profession which she practices and whether it concurs with her singularity or not. Everywhere she meets with a human being, she will find opportunity to sustain, to counsel, to help. If the factory worker or the office employee would only pay attention to the spirits of the persons who work with her in the same room, she would prevail upon trouble-laden hearts to be opened to her through a friendly word, a sympathetic question; she will find out where the shoe is pinching and will be able to provide relief. A need for maternal sympathy and help exists everywhere, and thus we are able to recapitulate in the one word "motherliness" that which we have developed as the characteristic value of woman. Only, this motherliness must not remain within the narrow circle of blood relations or of personal friends; but in accordance with the model of the Mother of Mercy, it must have its root in universal divine love for all who are there, belabored and burdened.

Thus I can summarize that a high vocation is designated in feminine singularity – that is, to bring true humanity in oneself and in others to development. But hazardous germs also lie in feminine singularity which endanger the essential value in its development and thereby the realization of mission. The dangers can only be conquered through rigorous discipline in the school of work and through the liberating power of divine grace. Our mission is to become flexible instruments in

God's hand and to effect his work, to which he leads us. If we fulfill our mission, we do what is best for ourselves, for our immediate environment, and together with it, what is best for the entire nation.

PART
V

A World in Flames

20

Holy Resistance

In early 1933, the Nazi Party amassed significant political power. In April, the same month that anti-Semitic legislation mandated Edith Stein's removal from her public teaching position, she penned this letter to Pope Pius XI.

Holy Father!

As a child of the Jewish people who, by the grace of God, for the past eleven years has also been a child of the Catholic Church, I dare to speak to the Father of Christianity about that which oppresses millions of Germans. For weeks we have seen deeds perpetrated in Germany that mock any sense of justice and humanity, not to mention love of neighbor. For years the leaders of National Socialism have been preaching hatred of the Jews. Now that they have seized the power of government and armed their followers, among them proven criminal elements, this seed of hatred has germinated. The government has only recently admitted that excesses have occurred. To what extent, we cannot tell, because public opinion is being gagged. However, judging by what I have learned through personal connections, it is in no way a matter of singular exceptional cases. Under pressure from reactions abroad, the government has turned to "milder" methods. It has issued the watchword, "No Jew shall have even one hair on his head harmed." But through boycott measures – by robbing people of their livelihood, civic honor, and fatherland – it drives many to desperation; within the last week, through private reports I was informed of five cases of suicide as a consequence of these hostilities. I am convinced that this is a general condition that will claim many more victims. One may regret that these unhappy people do not have greater inner strength to bear their misfortune. But the responsibility must fall, after all, on those who brought them to this point. It also falls on those who keep silent in the face of such happenings.

Everything that has happened and continues to happen on a daily basis originates with a government that calls itself "Christian." For weeks, not only Jews but also thousands of faithful Catholics in Germany, and, I believe, all over the world, have been waiting and hoping for the Church of Christ to raise its voice to put a stop to this abuse of Christ's name. Isn't this idolization of race and governmental power, which is being pounded into the public consciousness by the radio, open heresy? Isn't the effort to destroy Jewish blood an abuse of the holiest humanity of our Savior, of the most blessed Virgin, and the apostles? Isn't all this diametrically opposed to the conduct of our Lord and Savior, who, even on the cross, still prayed for his persecutors? And isn't this a black mark on the record of this Holy Year, which was intended to be a year of peace and reconciliation?

We all, who are faithful children of the Church and who see the conditions in Germany with open eyes, fear the worst for the prestige of the Church if the silence continues any longer. We are convinced that this silence will not be able in the long run to purchase peace with the present German government. For the time being, the fight against Catholicism will be conducted quietly and less brutally than against Jewry, but no less systematically. Before long, no Catholic will be able to hold office in Germany unless he dedicates himself unconditionally to the new course of action.

At the feet of your Holiness, requesting your apostolic blessing,

Dr. Edith Stein, Instructor at the German Institute for Scientific Pedagogy, Münster, Collegium Marianum.

21

The Way of the Cross

By November 1934, Edith Stein had lived behind convent walls for just over a year. In her essay "Love of the Cross," she looks to the power of the cross and the promise of the Christian faith in the context of worsening political conditions around her.

THE SIGHT OF THE WORLD in which we live, the need and misery, and the abyss of human malice, again and again dampens jubilation over the victory of light. The world is still deluged by mire, and still only a small flock has escaped from it to the highest mountain peaks. The battle between Christ and the Antichrist is not yet over. The followers of Christ have their place in this battle, and their chief weapon is the cross.

What does this mean? The burden of the cross that Christ assumed is that of corrupted human nature, with all its consequences in sin and suffering to which fallen humanity is subject. The meaning of the way of the cross is to carry this burden out of the world. The restoration of freed humanity to the heart of the heavenly Father, taking on the status of a child, is the free gift of grace, of merciful love. But this may not occur at the expense of divine holiness and justice. The entire sum of human failures from the first Fall up to the Day of Judgment must be blotted out by a corresponding measure of expiation. The way of the cross is this expiation. Jesus' triple collapse under the burden of the cross corresponds to the triple fall of humanity: the first sin, the rejection of the Savior by his chosen people, and the falling away of those who bear the name of Christian.

The Savior is not alone on the way of the cross. Not only are there adversaries around him who oppress him, but there are also people who succor him. The archetype of followers of the cross for all time is the Mother of God. Typical of those who submit to the suffering inflicted on them and experience Christ's blessing by bearing the cross is Simon of Cyrene. Representative of those who love the Lord and yearn to serve him is Veronica. Everyone who, in the course of time, has borne an onerous destiny in remembrance of the suffering Savior, or who has freely taken up works of expiation, has, by doing so, canceled some of the mighty load of human sin and has helped the Lord carry his burden.

Or rather, Christ the Head effects expiation in these members of his mystical body who put themselves, body and soul, at his disposal for carrying out his work of salvation. We can assume that the prospect of the faithful who would follow him on his way of the cross strengthened the Savior during his night on the Mount of Olives. And the strength of these cross-bearers helps him each time he falls. The righteous under the Old Covenant accompany him on the stretch of the way from the first to the second collapse. The disciples, both men and women, who surrounded him during his earthly life, assist him on the second stretch. The lovers of the cross whom he has awakened and will always continue to awaken anew in the changeable history of the struggling church: these are his allies at the end of time. We, too, are called for that purpose.

BUT BECAUSE *being* one with Christ is our sanctity, and progressively *becoming* one with him is our happiness on earth, the love of the cross in no way contradicts being a joyful child of God. Helping Christ carry his cross fills one with a strong and pure joy, and those who may and can do so – the builders of God's kingdom – are the most authentic children of God. And so those who have a predilection for the way of the cross by no means deny that Good Friday is past and that the work of salvation has been accomplished. Only those who are saved, only children of grace, can in fact be bearers of Christ's cross.

Only in union with the divine Head does human suffering take on expiatory power. To suffer and to be happy although suffering, to have one's feet on the earth, to walk on the dirty and rough paths of this earth and yet to be enthroned with Christ at the Father's right hand, to laugh and cry with the children of this world and ceaselessly sing the praises of God with the choirs of angels – this is the life of the Christian until the morning of eternity breaks forth.

22

The World Is in Flames

On New Year's Eve 1938, Edith Stein was smuggled into the Netherlands for her safety. On September 14, 1939, two weeks after Germany invaded Poland and started World War II, she wrote the following to encourage her fellow sisters to deeper faith and hope in the fire-quenching love of God.

"HAIL, CROSS, our only hope!" – this is what the holy church summons us to exclaim during the time for contemplating the bitter suffering of our Lord Jesus Christ. . . .

The Savior looks at us today, solemnly probing us, and asks each one of us: Will you remain faithful to the Crucified? Consider carefully! The world is in flames, the battle between Christ and the Antichrist has broken into the open. If you decide for Christ, it could cost you your life. Carefully consider what you promise. Taking and renewing vows is a dreadfully serious business. You make a promise to the Lord of heaven and earth. If you are not deadly serious about your will to fulfill it, you fall into the hands of the living God.

Before you hangs the Savior on the cross, because he became *obedient* unto death on the cross. He came into the world not to do his own will, but his Father's will. If you intend to be the bride of the Crucified, you too must completely renounce your own will and no longer have any desire except to fulfill God's will. He speaks to you in the holy Rule and the Constitutions of the Order. He speaks to you through the mouth of your superiors. He speaks to you by the gentle breath of the Holy Spirit in the depths of your heart. To remain true to your vow of obedience, you must listen to this voice day and night and follow its orders. However, this means daily and hourly crucifying your self-will and self-love.

The Savior hangs naked and destitute before you on the cross because he has chosen poverty. Those who want to follow him must renounce all earthly goods. It is not enough that you once left everything out there and came to the monastery. You must be serious about it now as well. Gratefully receive what God's providence sends you. Joyfully do without what he may let you be without. Do not be concerned with your own body, with its trivial necessities and inclinations, but leave concern to those who are entrusted with it. Do not be concerned about the coming day and the coming meal.

The Savior hangs before you with a pierced heart. He has spilled his heart's blood to win your heart. If you want to follow him in holy purity, your heart must be free of every earthly desire. Jesus, the Crucified, is to be the only object of your longings, your wishes, your thoughts.

Are you now alarmed by the immensity of what the holy vows require of you? You need not be alarmed. What you have promised is indeed beyond your own weak, human power. But it is not beyond the power of the Almighty – this power will become yours if you entrust yourself to him, if he accepts your pledge of troth. He does so on the day of your holy profession and will do it anew today. The loving heart of your Savior invites you to follow. It demands your obedience because the human will is blind and weak. Your will cannot find the way until it surrenders itself entirely to the divine will. He demands poverty because hands must be empty of earth's goods to receive the goods of heaven. He demands chastity because only the heart detached from all earthly love is free for the love of God. The arms of the Crucified are spread out to draw you to his heart. He wants your life in order to give you his.

Ave Crux, Spes unica! Hail, cross, our only hope!

The world is in flames. The conflagration can also reach our house. But high above all flames towers the cross. They cannot consume it. It is the path from earth to heaven. It will lift the one who embraces it in faith, love, and hope into the bosom of the Trinity. The world is in flames. Are you impelled to put them out? Look at the cross. From the open heart gushes the blood of the Savior. This extinguishes the flames of hell. Make your heart free by the faithful fulfillment of your vows; then the flood of divine love will be poured into your heart until it overflows and becomes fruitful to all the ends of the earth. Do you hear the groans of the wounded on the battlefields in the west and the east? You are not a physician and not a nurse and cannot bind up the wounds. You are enclosed in a cell and cannot get to them. Do you hear the anguish of the dying? You would like to be a priest and comfort them. Does the lament of the widows and orphans distress you? You would like to be an angel of mercy and help them. Look at the Crucified. If you are bound to him as a bride by the faithful observance of your holy vows, your being is precious blood. Bound to him, you are omnipresent as he is. You cannot help here or there like the physician, the nurse, or the priest. But you can be at all fronts, wherever there is grief, in the power of the cross. Your compassionate love takes you everywhere, this love from the divine heart. Its precious blood is poured everywhere – soothing, healing, saving.

The eyes of the Crucified look down on you – asking, probing. Will you make your covenant with the Crucified anew in all seriousness? What will you answer him? "Lord, to whom shall we go? You have the words of eternal life" (John 6:68).

Ave Crux, Spes unica!

23

I Will Remain with You

In this undated poem, written in 1938 at the latest, Edith Stein opens a window into her personal relationship with God. In the end, even for the philosopher, "All we can do is be amazed and stammer and fall silent / Because intellect and words fail."

You reign at the Father's right hand
In the kingdom of his eternal glory
As God's Word from the beginning.

You reign on the Almighty's throne
Also in transfigured human form,
Ever since the completion of your work on earth.

I believe this because your word teaches me so,
And because I believe, I know it gives me joy,
And blessed hope blooms forth from it.

A Sure Way

For where you are, there also are your own,
Heaven is my glorious homeland,
I share with you the Father's throne.

The Eternal who made all creatures,
Who, thrice holy, encompasses all being,
In addition has a silent, special kingdom of his own.

The innermost chamber of the human soul
Is the Trinity's favorite place to be,
His heavenly throne on earth.

To deliver this heavenly kingdom from the hand
of the enemy,
The Son of God has come as Son of Man,
He gave his blood as the price of deliverance.

In the heart of Jesus, which was pierced,
The kingdom of heaven and the land of earth
are bound together.
Here is for us the source of life.

This heart is the heart of the triune Divinity,
And the center of all human hearts
That bestows on us the life of God.

It draws us to itself with secret power,
It conceals us in itself in the Father's bosom
And floods us with the Holy Spirit.

This Heart, it beats for us in a small tabernacle
Where it remains mysteriously hidden
In that still, white host.

That is your royal throne on earth, O Lord,
Which visibly you have erected for us,
And you are pleased when I approach it.

Full of love, you sink your gaze into mine
And bend your ear to my quiet words
And deeply fill my heart with peace.

Yet your love is not satisfied
With this exchange that could still lead to separation:
Your heart requires more.

You come to me as early morning's meal each daybreak.
Your flesh and blood become food and drink for me
And something wonderful happens.

Your body mysteriously permeates mine
And your soul unites with mine:
I am no longer what once I was.

A Sure Way

You come and go, but the seed
That you sowed for future glory remains behind
Buried in this body of dust.

A luster of heaven remains in the soul,
A deep glow remains in the eyes,
A soaring in the tone of voice.

There remains the bond that binds heart to heart,
The stream of life that springs from yours
And animates each limb.

How wonderful are your gracious wonders!
All we can do is be amazed and stammer and fall silent
Because intellect and words fail.

Sources

Baird, Mary Julian. *Edith Stein and the Mother of God*. Marian Library Publications, 1959.

Stein, Edith. *Essays on Woman*. Edited by Lucy Gelber and Romaeus Leuven. Translated by Freda Mary Oben. ICS Publications, 1996.

Stein, Edith. *Finite and Eternal Being: An Attempt at an Ascent to the Meaning of Being.* Translated by Kurt F. Reinhardt. ICS Publications, 2002.

Stein, Edith. *Geistliche Texte II*. Herder Verlag, 2007.

Stein, Edith. *The Hidden Life: Hagiographic Essays, Meditations, Spiritual Texts*. Edited by Lucy Gelber and Michael Linssen. Translated by Waltraut Stein. ICS Publications, 1992.

Stein, Edith. *Knowledge and Faith*. Translated by Walter Redmond. ICS Publications, 2000.

Stein, Edith. *Life in a Jewish Family 1891–1916: An Autobiography.* ICS Publications, 1986.

Stein, Edith. *The Mystery of Christmas: Incarnation and Humanity.* Translated by Josephine Rucker. Darlington Carmel, 1985.

Stein, Edith. *The Science of the Cross*. Translated by Josephine Koeppel. ICS Publications, 2003.

Notes

Who Was Edith Stein?

Opening quote from *The Hidden Life* (see Chapter 22 below). Other Edith Stein quotes from *Life in a Jewish Family*.

1. **Approaching God**
   From "Ways to Know God" in *Knowledge and Faith*, 192–199.

2. **Standing Before God**
   From "Ways to Know God" in *Knowledge and Faith*, 183–190.

3. **The Soul's Way to God**
   From "The Cross and the Night" in *The Science of the Cross*, 91–93.

4. **Hidden in God**
   From "The Prayer of the Church" in *The Hidden Life*, 7–17.

5. **On Christian Philosophy**
   From "Is There a Christian Philosophy?" in *Finite and Eternal Being*, 22–29.

6. **Juxta Crucem Tecum Stare**
   "Juxta Crucem Tecum Stare!" in *Edith Stein and the Mother of God*, 7.

7. **The Meaning of the Cross**
   From "Introduction" and "The Message of the Cross" in *The Science of the Cross*, 9–11, 17–22.

8. **Signum Crucis**
   "Signum Crucis," translated by Carolyn Beard. German original: "Signum Crucis," in *Geistliche Texte II*, 47–49.

9. **The Dark Night of the Soul**
From "The Cross and the Night" and "Taking Up One's Cross" in *The Science of the Cross*, 39–54.

10. **The Night of Faith**
From "Taking Up One's Cross" in *The Science of the Cross*, 45–61.

11. **Easter Morning**
"Easter Morning," translated by Carolyn Beard. German original: "Ostermorgen," in *Geistliche Texte II*, 168–169.

12. **The Mystery of Sacrifice**
From "The Mystical Body of Christ" and "Means of Salvation" in *The Mystery of Christmas*, 13–22.

13. **The Holy Face**
"The Holy Face," translated by Carolyn Beard. German original: "Adventssonntag: Das heilige Antlitz," in *Geistliche Texte II*, 49–51.

14. **Hidden Life and Epiphany**
From "The Hidden Life and Epiphany" in *The Hidden Life*, 109–112.

15. **Holy Night**
"Holy Night," translated by Carolyn Beard. German original: "Heilige Nacht," in *Geistliche Texte II*, 51–53.

16. **The Summons of Christmas**
From "Advent and Christmas," "The Followers of the Incarnate Son of God," and "The Mystical Body of Christ" in *The Mystery of Christmas*, 4–14.

17. **The Soul of Woman**
From "Spirituality of the Christian Woman" in *Essays on Woman*, 82–95.

18. **Male and Female in the Image of God**
From "Spirituality of the Christian Woman" in *Essays on Woman*, 107–108.

19. **Women's Destiny**
From "The Significance of Woman's Intrinsic Value in National Life" in *Essays on Woman*, 217–224.

20. **Holy Resistance**
Text of Stein's 1933 letter to Pope Pius XI.

21. **The Way of the Cross**
From "Love of the Cross: Some Thoughts for the Feast of St. John of the Cross" in *The Hidden Life*, 91–93.

22. **The World Is in Flames**
"Elevation of the Cross, September 14, 1939: *Ave Crux, Spes Unica!*" in *The Hidden Life*, 94–97.

23. **I Will Remain with You**
Undated poem published in *The Hidden Life*, 134–139.

Plough Spiritual Guides

Love in the Void
Where God Finds Us
Simone Weil

Thunder in the Soul
To Be Known by God
Abraham Joshua Heschel

The Reckless Way of Love
Notes on Following Jesus
Dorothy Day

That Way and No Other
Following God Through Storm and Drought
By Amy Carmichael

Nothing Can Separate Us
Healing for Souls and Nations
Howard Thurman

Jesus Changes Everything
A New World Made Possible
Stanley Hauerwas

The Scandal of Redemption
When God Liberates the Poor, Saves Sinners, and Heals Nations
Oscar Romero

The Inconvenient Gospel
A Southern Prophet Tackles War, Wealth, Race, and Religion
Clarence Jordan

The Prayer God Answers
By Eberhard Arnold and Richard J. Foster

Why We Live in Community
Eberhard Arnold and Thomas Merton

Plough Publishing House
845-572-3455 • info@plough.com
PO BOX 398, Walden, NY 12586, USA
Robertsbridge, East Sussex TN32 5DR, UK
4188 Gwydir Highway, Elsmore, NSW 2360, Australia
www.plough.com